T0299225

"Over the last ten years, Ethereum has transformed from being a whitepaper describing a proposal for a more general-purpose block-chain into a highly diverse and complex ecosystem. *Absolute Essentials of Ethereum* does an excellent job describing the basics, both of the technology and of how people maintain and use it and where it's going in the years to come."

Vitalik Buterin, *Founder of Ethereum*

"Since its origins as a world computer, Ethereum has gone on to become a world-wide phenomenon. Over that time, to those on the inside, it feels like decades have passed. Paul is one of the few people with the ability to simply and modestly merge those years of collective coordination into a meaningful history of what Ethereum is and more importantly why it matters. I'd highly recommend this book to anyone looking to get caught up and involved in the Ethereum ecosystem."

Scott Moore, *Co-founder of Gitcoin*

"This is the perfect text for anyone to get up to speed with Ethereum and its key concepts. Written in a highly personable and engaging style, this book will take both the technical and non-technical reader on a tour of the most important moments in Ethereum's history and its most significant projects."

Nick Almond (Dr), *Founder of Factory DAO*

"A well-written, comprehensive introduction to the various compo-nent sectors of Ethereum. This book appeals to both readers completely new to Ethereum and those old hands trying to remember the historical developments leading to the current state of affairs."

Laurence E. Day (Dr), *Founder of Wildcat Finance and Advisor to Euler Finance*

Absolute Essentials of Ethereum

Absolute Essentials of Ethereum is a concise textbook which guides the reader through the fascinating world of the emerging Ethereum ecosystem, from the basics of how its blockchain works to cutting-edge applications.

Written by an experienced educator, each chapter is designed to progress potential students from class to class. Technical concepts are clearly explained for those new to the topic and readers are supported with definitions and summaries in each chapter. Real-life case studies situate the overviews in a contemporary context. Topics covered include the Ethereum Execution and Consensus layers, Ethereum governance and community, Decentralised Autonomous Organisations (DAOs), Decentralised Finance (DeFi), Non-Fungible Tokens (NFTs) and Layer 2.

This book is the ideal text to support undergraduate and postgraduate courses on blockchain technologies, cryptocurrencies, Web3 and fintech, as well as for those who want to know how Ethereum really works.

Dr. Paul Dylan-Ennis is Lecturer/Assistant Professor in the College of Business, University College Dublin. His research focuses on the cultural and social aspects of the Ethereum blockchain and the wider Web3 ecosystem.

Absolute Essentials of Business and Economics

Textbooks are an extraordinarily useful tool for students and teachers, as is demonstrated by their continued use in the classroom and online. Successful textbooks run into multiple editions, and in endeavouring to keep up with developments in the field, it can be difficult to avoid increasing length and complexity.

This series of Shortform textbooks offers a range of books which zero-in on the absolute essentials. In focusing on only the core elements of each sub-discipline, the books provide a useful alternative or supplement to traditional textbooks.

Absolute Essentials of Business Behavioural Ethics
Nina Seppala

Absolute Essentials of Corporate Governance
Stephen Bloomfield

Absolute Essentials of Business Ethics
Peter A. Stanwick & Sarah D. Stanwick

Absolute Essentials of Creative Thinking and Problem Solving
Tony Proctor

Absolute Essentials of Environmental Economics
Barry C. Field

Absolute Essentials of Marketing Research
Bonita M. Kolb

Absolute Essentials of Advertising
Sarah Turnbull

Absolute Essentials of Ethereum
Paul Dylan-Ennis

For more information about this series, please visit: www.routledge.com/
Absolute-Essentials-of-Business-and-Economics/book-series/ABSOLUTE

Absolute Essentials of Ethereum

Paul Dylan-Ennis

Routledge
Taylor & Francis Group

LONDON AND NEW YORK

First published 2024
by Routledge
4 Park Square, Milton Park, Abingdon, Oxon OX14 4RN

and by Routledge
605 Third Avenue, New York, NY 10158

Routledge is an imprint of the Taylor & Francis Group, an informa business

© 2024 Paul Dylan-Ennis

British Library Cataloguing-in-Publication Data
A catalogue record for this book is available from the British Library

Library of Congress Cataloguing-in-Publication Data
Names: Dylan-Ennis, Paul, author.
Title: Absolute essentials of ethereum / Paul Dylan-Ennis.
Description: Abingdon, Oxon ; New York, NY : Routledge, 2024. |
Series: Routledge absolute essentials in business and economics |
Includes bibliographical references and index.
Identifiers: LCCN 2023048174 | ISBN 9781032334189 (hbk) | ISBN
9781032334202 (pbk) | ISBN 9781003319603 (ebk)
Subjects: LCSH: Ethereum (Databases) | Blockchains (Databases) |
Cryptocurrencies.
Classification: LCC QA76.546.E84 D95 2024 | DDC 332.4--dc23/
eng/20231026
LC record available at https://lccn.loc.gov/2023048174

ISBN: 978-1-032-33418-9 (hbk)
ISBN: 978-1-032-33420-2 (pbk)
ISBN: 978-1-003-31960-3 (ebk)

DOI: 10.4324/9781003319603

Typeset in Times New Roman
by MPS Limited, Dehradun

Contents

Preface

In a phrase, Ethereum is a world computer. You could happily use Ethereum for many years and never really understand what that means. In fact, that's how countless people use it today. And that's ultimately the aim. In the future, the Ethereum world computer should be as invisible as the Internet is. We all use the Internet, but could you explain what it is, *really*? No matter, so long as it works. The idea is that people will use what are known as Decentralised Applications (dApps) and never think about what makes them run, Ethereum. Some of us, unfortunate souls that we are, nonetheless have to know how things work. This book is for people who want to know their Externally-Owned Account from their contract account, their world state from their Beacon state, their fungible from non-fungible token. It will suit if you are a newcomer who knows little more than the name Ethereum. It should also suit if you are quite familiar with the everyday drama surrounding Ethereum, but never took the time to learn the nuts and bolts and felt you were missing out by not doing so. Advanced readers might enjoy spotting what parts I had to omit to fit the remit of the absolute essentials of Ethereum.

The book should slot well into a University class on Ethereum, especially since these days Ethereum is more or less synonymous with the industry variously known as cryptocurrency, Crypto, blockchain, Web3 and the latest addition, onchain. The reason I wrote this book is so I could assign the chapters to my own students. For my sins, I have been teaching about Bitcoin and Ethereum since 2016 at University College Dublin. I even created the first Ethereum-specific module, called "The Ethereum Ecosystem" (do forgive the humble brag, it's the only time I've been first). For a long time, the industry could be captured by assigning academic articles to students. But in the last few years, especially since 2021, Ethereum in particular has sprawled and sprawled. That's exciting and healthy for the Ethereum ecosystem, but the academic literature has not kept pace. I simply couldn't find generalist articles suitable to assign to students. That's no fault of academics, who need to specialise, but it became a problem because I had to wedge in articles I was not quite happy with. Then the horror dawned on me. I'll have to write a book to fix my own problem.

OK, some cold, hard truths. Ethereum is a complicated beast. I could lie to you and pretend otherwise, but you'll find out it's true soon enough. At root, Ethereum is essentially a giant software experiment involving many thousands of researchers and developers contributing to the upkeep of a world computer. The computer is unlike any other you know. It's hosted on thousands of software clients, called full nodes, run by true believers (including myself). In the first three chapters, we tackle the hard bits, Ethereum's Central Processing Unit (CPU), called the Ethereum Virtual Machine (EVM), and Ethereum's hard drive, its blockchain. Once we've got a handle on how Ethereum works as an infrastructure, we'll switch a little to how Ethereum is governed, because Ethereum is, at heart, a social project constituted by real people. We'll then do a speed run through what I consider the trifecta of Decentralised Application (dApp) primitives that capture the attention of everyday users: Decentralised Autonomous Organisations (DAOs), Decentralised Finance (DeFi) and Non-Fungible Tokens (NFTs). While these sound intimidating in the abstract, they are really just blockchain communities into self-organising, finance or creativity. In the last chapter, I let loose a bit and introduce the advanced frontier of Ethereum research and development.

Acknowledgements

This book is dedicated to my parents, Tony and Triona, and to my brothers and sisters, Lisa, Colm, Niki and Ciara. Most importantly, it is dedicated to my grandfather, John Moran, who instilled a love of learning in me by bringing me to the library in Walkinstown as a child.

A book on Ethereum is not possible without input from the Ethereum hivemind. I stand on the shoulders of what was once known as Crypto Twitter (now "X") and the small but growing body of Ethereum academic researchers. I am sure to have overlooked many people. To those, I apologise.

Tara Merk, Donncha Kavanagh, Rachel-Rose O'Leary, Quinn DuPont, Dennis Pourteaux, Brady Dale, Wong Joon Ian, Daniel Kuhn, Stefan Deleveaux, Chase Chapman, Ann Brody, Sacha Yves Saint-Léger, Andrew Thurman, David Z. Morris, Nick Almond, Lani Trock, Manu Alzuru, Gabriel Haines, Laura Winn, Amir Taaki, Jordan McKinney, Vitalik Buterin, Ben Edgington, Trent Van Epps, Mario Havel, Tim Beiko, Scott Moore, Kevin Owocki, Laurence E. Day, Troy Cross, Craig Warmke, Andrew Bailey, Alex Gladstein, Morshed Mannan, Primavera De Filippi, Kelsie Nabben, Samantha Yap, Pooja Ranjan, Gianluca Miscione, Séamas Kelly, Lory Kehoe, Reuben Godfrey. And finally Anthony Sassano's *The Daily Gwei* and David Hoffman and Ryan Sean Adams' *Bankless* for keeping me up to date.

Finally, to Satoshi Nakamoto, wherever you are, for providing direction when all direction seemed lost.

1 Introducing Ethereum

Ethereum is a computing platform for decentralised applications. It is often called the world computer. It is a computer in the sense that it acts as a platform to enable applications, like how your laptop is a computer that enables you to play games or write essays. Developers create applications that run on this computer and then the everyday Ethereum user interacts with them. This would not be impressive on its own, but Ethereum is not owned or run by a company, like Google or Amazon. Instead, Ethereum is a world computer hosted by volunteers all over the world. These volunteers are collectively hosting the current state of the Ethereum computer and then updating it as new events occur. This is enabled by the Ethereum Virtual Machine (EVM), Ethereum's processing "brain" and Ethereum's blockchain, called the Beacon Chain, a secure record-keeping system that allows people who do not know each other to coordinate and reach agreement. Ethereum is the cumulative effort of an open-source community to provide an open and transparent world computer that anyone can leverage. Since its launch on July 31, 2015, people have used Ethereum to create entirely novel applications primitives in the areas of organisation, finance and creativity.

The story of Ethereum begins with the story of Vitalik Buterin, its creator and his interest in the original blockchain implementation, Bitcoin.[1] Bitcoin is a blockchain designed to securely track a currency, called bitcoins. Buterin had been a member of the Bitcoin community since March 2011, aged just 17. He started out as a blogger for *Bitcoin Weekly* and then collaborated in August 2011 with Mihai Alisie to create *Bitcoin Magazine*, now ironically an outlet that discourages the use of alternatives to Bitcoin, including Ethereum! Buterin became known for writing technically informed but accessible articles on Bitcoin, but also showed a keen interest in how the blockchain concept could be extended beyond money.

By late 2013, when Ethereum was conceived, people had started to ponder whether the blockchain concept pioneered by Bitcoin might be

DOI: 10.4324/9781003319603-1

extended into fresh directions.[2] In late November 2013, Buterin turned his attention toward creating the Ethereum white paper. In blockchain cultures, a white paper is a conceptual paper outlining the core ideas and vision for a blockchain project. The white paper template is derived from Satoshi Nakamoto's original Bitcoin white paper. On November 27, 2013, Buterin, aged 19, sent the earliest version of the white paper to 13 developers entitled "Introducing Ethereum: a generalized smart contract/DAC platform." The final "canonical" version bears the title "Ethereum: A Next Generation Smart Contract and Decentralized Application Platform." The nascent Ethereum team first spent some time in a hacker house in Miami and then announced Ethereum on January 26, 2014, at the Bitcoin Miami conference.

What Is Ethereum?

Ethereum is, at heart, users running software that connects them to the Ethereum Peer-to-Peer (P2P) network. *Peer-to-Peer (P2P) networking* is a technique where individual computers, known as nodes, connect with other computers that follow a shared protocol, forming a network. By analogy, the Internet is a vast network of computers and applications all following the Transmission Control Protocol/Internet Protocol (TCP/IP) for transmitting data to one another. Because they follow the same protocol they can communicate with each other. In Ethereum, the nodes in the network are all following the *Ethereum protocol*, an overarching name for the various technical specifications found in Ethereum.[3] In Ethereum's case, the network exists to host a shared world computer. In a Peer-to-Peer (P2P) network like Ethereum, there is no central node (Figure 1.1). Everything that happens must be done as a collective effort, in a decentralised manner.

There is the mainnet or live implementation of the Ethereum network, the Ethereum Mainnet, and there are also testnets where developers can experiment, such as Sepolia. The connection to the Ethereum Mainnet and testnets is made by running Ethereum software. This software must be compatible with the Ethereum protocol. Here we need to emphasise that there are different kinds of users of Ethereum. First, Ethereum has power users known as full nodes. Ethereum *full nodes* process for validate transactions and keep a history of the Ethereum blockchain record. Many are also involved in helping to update the current state of Ethereum through a process called staking (a future topic). These users are the backbone of the Ethereum network. As long as full node users run Ethereum software, Ethereum exists.

Second, we have everyday users who use Ethereum wallet software. An *Ethereum wallet* is software allowing Ethereum users to manage an account or wallet (both common terms). These wallets and services rely on full nodes,

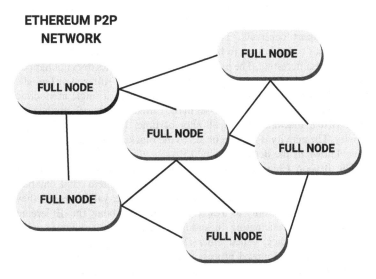

Figure 1.1 Ethereum P2P network.

which means they are less independent than full nodes, but they don't require the user to process transactions or host the blockchain, making them far less resource-intensive. The most popular choices are browser-based wallets like MetaMask, desktop wallets such as Frame, mobile wallets such as Status and hardware wallets such as Trezor. Browser and mobile-based wallets are known as hot wallets because they connect to the Internet, exposing them to threats, but hardware wallets are known as cold wallets, because they are offline, making them harder to target. Many users host their funds on exchanges, but this practice is strongly discouraged as it is relatively common for exchanges to be hacked or collapse.

When a user downloads Ethereum software an identity is created for them, but it is not their real-world identity. Instead, Ethereum software generates an Ethereum account with an associated pseudonym. A second type of account exists, called a contract account. These accounts contain the code of programs called smart contracts that users can interact with and are originally created by developers. The processing of user activity and contract interactions is done by the Ethereum Virtual Machine (EVM).

The *Ethereum Virtual Machine (EVM)* is the Central Processing Unit (CPU) that coordinates the transition of the Ethereum world computer from state to state. The Ethereum state is a large collection of accounts, both user and application accounts. It represents the current status or state of affairs of the world computer. Users can make transactions to either send Ethereum's native currency called ether (ETH) or they can interact with the smart contracts. This can mean anything from organising communities to buying art to borrowing and lending assets. Now here is where it gets interesting. The processing of these activities does not happen on a centralised computer in a data centre owned by Amazon or Google. The EVM does not exist somewhere "out there" as a single monolithic computer, but instead, the full nodes in the Ethereum network emulate the same virtual machine in a small slice of time, 12 seconds, to process activity. The activity is then recorded to the blockchain, Ethereum's hard drive, known as the Beacon Chain.

The Beacon Chain keep track of the world computer's history. A *blockchain* is a secure digital record-keeping system that enables decentralised coordination among users. Ethereum validators, as they are known, collaborate to reach a consensus about the Ethereum blockchain by participating in staking. Staking sees validators stake Ethereum's currency, called ether (ETH), for a right to update the blockchain. A randomised process chooses one participant in a slot to update the blockchain's state. If they misbehave they lose some of their stake, but if they play honestly they are rewarded.

Heavy stuff, I know! The new terminology is relentless and the concepts unforgiving because they run counter to how we normally think. But remember, many people who use Ethereum don't know how it works and they get on just fine. You know how to use your laptop, but likely have little to no idea how it *really* works. What this book will do is de-mystify the explanation you just read bit by bit. By the end of the book, you'll be dropping these terms to confound newcomers like you always knew what they meant. We need to fake it until we make it for now, but we'll get there soon.

Technical Decentralisation

The question now becomes why does Ethereum use a blockchain rather than more traditional record-keeping systems, like a database? What does a blockchain add that attracts people to Ethereum? First, let's see what technical characteristics a blockchain has:

a Blockchains are *architecturally decentralised* or *distributed* among all full node participants, rather than located in a single place.
b Blockchains are *tamper resistant*, meaning nobody can unilaterally make changes to the history. Once a state of affairs is accepted it becomes permanent history and can't be reverted.
c Blockchains are *transparent*, meaning all activity that happens on a blockchain is completely public. This follows logically from (a).

I'll simply refer to all these characteristics together as *technical decentralisation*, since that is how blockchain communities generally think of them, as a set. Whenever I need to be more precise I will evoke the specific term from (a)–(c). The purpose of technical decentralisation in a blockchain is to remove the reliance on intermediaries known as trusted third parties. A *trusted third party* is an intermediary that users rely on to provide certain services. For example, consider the situation when I am using a banking application. The bank's database, its record-keeping system, is architecturally centralised. It is under the direct control of the system administrators. The bank's database is mutable or changeable. Your account might be frozen, transactions reverted or charges automatically made. The database is opaque and private. You don't know what is happening beyond what is presented to you in your account. There are good reasons for all of the above, but to understand why people desire blockchains we have to understand why trusted third parties can be a problem.

Trusted third parties are mistrusted in blockchain communities because they are centralised. *Centralisation* is the concentration of decision-making in an organisation or industry to a single authority or a small set of authorities. For instance, in a small organisation like a local football team, decision-making power might be under the control of a single person who badly mismanages it. In more complex cases, such as the banking industry, decision-making power is centralised under the control of a small number of banks and financial entities and their privileged position means they can deny banking to certain sectors of society, create monopolies, introduce punitive fees, etc. Or think about how the Internet today is dominated by centralised entities like social media companies that monetise our data (Meta, X), crowd out smaller vendors (Amazon) or determine what information we see (Google). To blockchain communities, centralisation appears to lead inevitably to a loss of autonomy and control. You will have to decide for yourself whether you believe in this premise, but it is foundational to blockchain cultures. The answer to centralisation is, naturally, decentralisation.

Political Decentralisation

Technical decentralisation ultimately exists to support *political decen-tralisation*, meaning a context where authority is spread among all participating members, rather than concentrated. Decentralisation, both technical and political, is the core principle of blockchain communities like Ethereum. In the absence of central authorities, politically decen-tralised communities rely on coordination and consensus mechanisms to reach agreement. In Ethereum, any changes to how the world computer operates can be made by anyone, but it must gain wide support from all stakeholders in the Ethereum ecosystem. The world computer is itself updated not by a central authority, but by a distributed network or validators who often know little to nothing about each other. Alongside decentralisation itself, politically decentralised communities are also committed to the principles of permissionlessness, censorship resistance and credible neutrality.

Permissionlessness: Blockchains do not require the permission of anyone to participate. If someone is able to download the blockchain's software, then they are free to join the network, no questions asked and to transact on it. There is no central authority or trusted third party to ask permission from.

Censorship resistance: In a blockchain context, nobody is in a position to unilaterally censor, block or reverse transactions. There is no central authority or trusted party that decides which transactions are legitimate or illegitimate. Therefore every transaction is equal in the eyes of the blockchain. We'll discuss in a future chapter an interesting case where Ethereum's censorship resistance has been tested.

Credible neutrality: Blockchains must be designed in a manner that does not favour one part of the blockchain community over another. The concept of credible neutrality, introduced by Ethereum's creator Vitalik Buterin, stresses that blockchains must have self-evident legitimacy, where everybody can easily recognise the intrinsic fairness of the protocol's design.

Overall we want our blockchain to be technically decentralised – architecturally decentralised, tamper resistant, transparent – and from here gain the politically decentralised properties of permissionlessness, censorship resistance and credible neutrality.

Blockchain implementations are technically and politically decentralised to the extent that centralised power is absent. When confused about a decision or action, just recall that there is usually an expectation to minimise centralisation and maximise decentralisation. When you encounter community friction, it will likely be due to a violation of the commitment to decentralisation. You should expect to find contradictions and paradoxes around centralisation and decentralisation. Like any human venture, there are the ideals a community holds and the accommodations people have made around them.

The Ethereum Ecosystem

We'll spend the first few chapters becoming familiar with Ethereum as a protocol, but it is important to keep in mind that Ethereum ultimately exists to support an ecosystem of decentralised applications. To capture this broader sense of Ethereum, it has become more and more common to refer to the Ethereum Ecosystem. The *Ethereum Ecosystem* is an umbrella term for all the activity that is built upon or associated with the Ethereum blockchain. In particular, Ethereum is powered by three application primitives that we will all get their own chapters in this book, but here I provide some quite basic definitions, so you can get a sense of where we are going long-term:

Decentralised Autonomous Organisations (DAOs): a set of coordination tools and techniques that combine to enable the decentralised management of organisations and communities.

Decentralised Finance (DeFi): financial applications that enable the trading of assets, lending, borrowing, liquidity provision, among others.

Non-Fungible Tokens (NFTs): applications that enable the creation and trading of blockchain-based artworks and collectibles.

I like to imagine the Ethereum Ecosystem as similar to a bustling cosmopolitan city. It has its own Town Hall (Decentralisation Autonomous Organisations), its own Wall Street (Decentralised Finance) and its own Bohemian art scene (Non-Fungible Tokens), but there's also a dangerous part of town to be avoided (the cybercriminals). What makes Ethereum fascinating, like London or New York, is that it caters to every taste. Ethereum carries a cosmopolitan or pluralist atmosphere that can be quite appealing, but like many an interesting city, you should keep your wits about you.

Notes

1 Despite its relative youth, the story of how Ethereum was created is surprisingly well-documented. There are three books that cover the period from first conception in November 2013 to Ethereum's launch on July 30, 2015: Russo's *The Infinite Machine* (2020), Leising's *Out of the Ether* (Leising, 2021) and Shin's *The Cryptopians* (Shin, 2022).
2 At the time, Buterin was engaged with two projects at the forefront of this approach, known as Bitcoin 2.0. The first was Colored Coins, who hired Buterin to create an updated white paper for them. Colored Coins allow users to tag small denominations of bitcoin with metadata. Once stamped with this metadata, these tagged bitcoins represent different assets, such as stocks, at least within the context of the Colored Coins community. The second project, Mastercoin, embedded simple contracts into small bitcoin transactions that would then be interpreted by the Mastercoin protocol. Mastercoin was primarily used to fundraise and create currencies at this early stage, but was intent on adding more features, which is what Buterin was investigating, specifically whether advanced financial contracts could be built there. In his work on both projects, while staying in Israel in October and early November 2013, Buterin had a breakthrough. In a proposal to the Mastercoin team, Buterin proposes that rather than extend Mastercoin feature by feature, it would make more sense to pursue a more generalised approach. Users could

use a simple programming language to create whatever *they* wished. The Mastercoin team did not bite, but the proposal proved the catalyst for Buterin to create his own blockchain implementation, Ethereum.

3 This is a little bit of a grey zone in Ethereum. There is not really a specific Ethereum protocol you can point to, but rather a set of specifications, some of which are partially outdated, some of which overlap. I've tried to subsume these various forms of documentation under a label, the Ethereum Protocol, because something like that does exist, but I'm taking a bit of pedagogical liberty by formalising it. I consider the protocol to encompass roughly: the original white paper by Vitalik Buterin, the more technical yellow paper by Gavin Wood, and then the execution layer and the consensus layer specs. There are currently efforts to update and standardise everything, such as the Ethereum Execution Layer Specification (EELS) update of the yellow paper, and likely in a few years, we'll see a more formal structure.

References

Leising M (2021) *Out of the Ether: The Amazing Story of Ethereum and the $55 Million Heist That Almost Destroyed It All*. New Jersey: John Wiley & Sons.

Russo C (2020) *The Infinite Machine*. New York: Harper Business.

Shin L (2022) *The Cryptopians: Idealism, Greed, Lies, and the Making of the First Big Cryptocurrency Craze*. New York: Public Affairs.

2 Ethereum

The Execution Layer (EL)

Ethereum is a decentralised world computer. The purpose of Ethereum is to act as a computing platform for Decentralised Applications (dApps). What makes Ethereum unique is that it is not controlled by a trusted third party, an intermediary that users trust to provide certain services, but instead by a global network of users called full nodes that cooperate to change the computer's state from one to another. It can be thought of as a shared computer in the cloud, not run by Google or Amazon, but by many thousands of distributed volunteers. Full nodes are users running Ethereum software clients that execute transactions and keep a copy of the computer's history, called a blockchain. To achieve this, an Ethereum full node has to run two pieces of software, an execution client and a consensus client. In this chapter, we're concerned with what happens in execution clients, at Ethereum's Execution Layer (EL). The *Execution Layer (EL)* names the part of the Ethereum protocol concerned with executing transactions and storing the world state. We will act throughout this chapter as an Ethereum full node because it gives us the most complete picture of Ethereum.

World State

Imagine we stopped the Ethereum world computer right now. The snapshot we would have at this particular slice in time is the world state. The world state is a database that maps addresses to user accounts and application accounts (Figure 2.1). More formally, Ethereum's *world state* is a database mapping Ethereum addresses to Externally-Owned Accounts (user accounts) and contract accounts (application accounts).[1] Whenever anything new happens the world state needs to be updated. If an Externally-Owned Account sends another Externally-Owned Account ETH then this changes the world state of Ethereum. If an EOA interacts with a contract account then this causes a change in the world state as well. The world state changes every 12 seconds based on all the transactions users initiate.

DOI: 10.4324/9781003319603-2

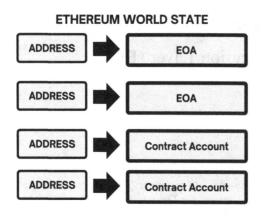

Figure 2.1 Ethereum world state.

Ethereum Accounts

Externally-Owned Accounts (EOA)

Externally-Owned Accounts (EOA) are user accounts that can create transactions and are controlled by private keys. An EOA is not associated with your real-world identity. Rather than using your actual identity, Ethereum software generates one for you, using Public Key Cryptography. *Public Key Cryptography* is used to establish pseudonymous identities in a blockchain implementation. Externally-Owned Accounts (EOAs) are managed using a keypair containing a private key and a public key, which have a cryptographic relationship. Private keys are *like* passwords in that they allow access to your Ethereum account and let you perform actions, such as sending a transaction or interacting with an application. Private keys should not be shared with anyone, ever. *Unlike* passwords, you are entirely responsible for your own private keys. If you misplace them, delete them or they are stolen then there is no recourse. An old Bitcoiner mantra: "Not your keys, not your coins."

In a more technical sense, an Ethereum account's private key is a 256-bit number (between 1 and 2^{256}). You can visualise this as a number range so astronomically large no two people will end up with the same number. To your computer, a 256-bit number is a long series of binary 0 s and 1 s, but this binary number gets translated for us into a more manageable hexadecimal form. Hexadecimal is a base-16 numbering system that uses 0–9 and A–F to representationally compress large binary numbers. Below is an Ethereum account's private key represented in hexadecimal:

a37efb76efceae747a746f64ef25f9f8f622f57d754f397705425dbe28f901b4

Most Ethereum wallets create what is known as a seed phrase that can be used to derive the private keys of multiple accounts. I know that sounds tricky, but in practical terms, it just means you won't encounter raw private keys much, but will instead encounter the seed phrase. Here is what one looks like:

heart forest bird damp abandon soap bird holiday poverty expire grant keep

The majority of Ethereum wallets will use a seed phrase from which you can derive many individual accounts. This means you can have a single seed phrase, but many derived accounts.

On the other side of the identity equation is the public key. In formal terms, a *public key* is a set of coordinates generated from the private key using Elliptic Curve Cryptography (ECC). The ECC algorithm is *one-way*. I can generate a public key from a private key and show you the public key, but you can't reverse engineer from the public key back to the private key.

Public Key Cryptography allows us to establish a digital signature scheme. A *digital signature* is a cryptographic signature appended to transactions using private keys. The public key can be used to verify the digital signature. Here's the digital signature scheme:

i Software creates the private key.
ii Software derives the public key from the private key.
iii User signs transactions with a digital signature using their private key.
iv Network verifies digital signature came from the private key using the public key.

Ethereum transactions are sent to Ethereum addresses. Informally, Ethereum addresses are identifiers for accounts. Formally, *Ethereum addresses* are 42-character hexadecimal identifiers derived from the last 20 bytes of the public key with a 0x prefix. An example address looks as follows:

0x5e16Fa36555B428823d3Ed32aa7CbB07a92F301B

In the Ethereum roadmap, there are plans to transition over to a more intuitive and user-friendly account experience called Account Abstraction. It might even exist by the time you are reading this.

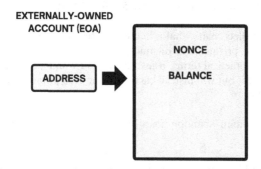

Figure 2.2 Externally-Owned Account.

The hope is Account Abstraction will give users more control and flexibility over their accounts, such as the social recovery of private keys.

Externally-Owned Accounts (EOA) have an Ethereum address and an associated account state.[2] EOAs contain two fields: the Nonce and the Balance. The *Nonce* in an Ethereum account is an incrementing number showing how many transactions an account has made and how many contracts it has created. The Nonce is used to determine the order of transactions in the same slot. The *Balance* is how much ETH the account is holding. We can extrapolate that tracking the world state is partially to track the current transaction count and balance of an EOA (Figure 2.2).

Contract Accounts

To understand contract accounts, we must first understand what contract accounts are for, namely smart contracts. Intuitively stated, smart contracts are programs that can run on Ethereum. You can think of them as computer programs that are designed with Ethereum's unique properties in mind. Within this context, what is attractive about a smart contract is we know a smart contract's code will always execute the same for everyone, making them deterministic. Deterministic means the same input for one user will produce the same result for another. This is the agreement or contract. Less intuitively stated, a *smart contract* is a set of instructions called Opcodes. An *Opcode* is an instruction or command to be processed by the Ethereum Virtual Machine (EVM) (more later). For example, the first three Opcodes are STOP (halt execution), ADD (addition operation) and MUL (multiplication). Smart contracts are written in high-level programming languages, custom to Ethereum, such as Solidity and Vyper. These are similar to the programming languages you might know already, like JavaScript or Python. Solidity is the most

CONTRACT ACCOUNT

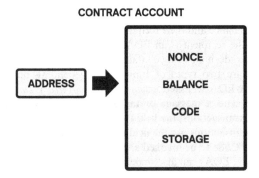

Figure 2.3 Contract account.

popular and I'll stick to it as the example. Solidity contract code gets compiled into EVM bytecode before it is deployed. *EVM bytecode* is the low-level programming language the Ethereum world computer can read and execute. This sounds complicated, but it just means developers write in more contextually-human high-level languages like Solidity, but the EVM reads and executes in the low-level "computer" language of EVM bytecode. The "byte" part of bytecode refers to how each Opcode instruction is a byte, a little chunk of data.[3]

Contract accounts are smart contracts that have been deployed on Ethereum and are controlled by their own internal code (Figure 2.3). Contract accounts have an Ethereum address and an associated account state. Contract accounts contain a state with four fields: the Nonce, the Balance, the Code and the Storage. The *Nonce* is an incrementing number showing how many contracts this contract account has created.[4] The *Balance* is how much ETH the contract account is holding. The *Code* is the smart contract code contained in the account. When a contract account is created, the smart contract Code is hashed and stored permanently on the blockchain, meaning it is immutable. Whenever an EOA triggers the contract account the Ethereum Virtual Machine (EVM) will pull up this code and run it, based on inputs from a transaction. Finally, contract accounts have Storage. The *Storage* maps the contents of the contract account. When a transaction involving a contract account is processed, the changes are recorded permanently in the contract's Storage.

Ethereum Transactions

There are two main types of transactions in Ethereum. The first is a Message Call. *Message Calls* from EOAs communicate a desired change in the Ethereum world state. The two change fields are Value and Input Data. With *Value*, an EOA sending ETH to another EOA is asking to update their account Balance and their recipients' account Balance in the world state, whether the recipient is an EOA or contract account. The *Input Data* field is a hexadecimal string containing information alongside a transaction. There are two types of Input Data depending on the transaction type. EOA-EOA transactions can include *arbitrary Data* in this field, perhaps to send a message or tag a transaction. However, usually in EOA-EOA transactions, the field is left empty. EOA-contract or contract-contract transactions use the field to include Input Data that includes the contract's Code to be invoked and any proposed changes to Storage. As a final note, EOAs can also make contract accounts interact with each other, but the initiating transaction must always originate from an EOA.

The second type of transaction is *Contract Creation,* which requests a new contract account to be added to the Ethereum world state. Contract creation transactions are sent to an empty address since there's no recipient. Their own contract addresses, once initialised, are a combination of the sender's address and the last Nonce from the sender's account.

Ether and Transaction Fees

The currency of the Ethereum blockchain is called ether and its ticker symbol is ETH (pronounced like the -eth in teeth). The currency unit is 1 ether (ETH) and it can be subdivided into wei, its smallest denomination:

wei	1
ada	10^3
babbage	10^6
shannon / gwei	10^9
szabo	10^{12}
finney	10^{15}
ether	10^{18}

Realistically, most people will only encounter wei, gwei and ether. Gwei is used to denominate transaction fees.

The Ethereum team decided to have a pre-sale of ETH.[5] The ETH pre-sale ran for 42 days (22nd July 2014 – 2nd September 2014) and investors could buy 2000 ETH for 1 BTC and then after 14 days 1337 ETH for 1 BTC. There were 60 million ETH available for investors to buy and then approximately 12 million set aside for co-founders, early contributors and the Ethereum Foundation, a non-profit dedicated to building the Ethereum ecosystem. The pre-sale raised approximately $18.3 million. At the time of writing, there are around 120 million ETH issued.

The practical purpose of ETH is to pay transaction fees. The following discussion refers to Ethereum transaction fees since August 2021 and the London Upgrade/EIP-1559. I stress this because you will often encounter online explanations that describe the pre-2021 situation.

To understand the transaction fee, we need to understand the distinction between gas cost and gas fees. In Ethereum, computational cycles are calculated in a unit called gas. A gas unit is not a currency unit. Gas cost relates only to how many computational cycles are needed. Every computational instruction (an Opcode) in a transaction has an associated *gas cost*. The most well-known is the cost of a transaction, 21,000 gas. However, interactions with contract accounts will involve further Opcode instructions and further gas costs. ADD costs 3 gas. DIV costs 5 gas. BALANCE costs 700 gas. And so on. When a user sends a transaction they include a Gas Limit. The *Gas Limit* is the maximum amount of gas, that is units of computation, a user is willing to pay for.

Each unit of gas I consume will incur a gas fee. *Gas fees* pay for gas units and are denominated in a small amount of ETH called gwei (one billion wei or 0.0000000001 ETH). Gas fees have two forms. The *base fee* refers to the algorithmically dynamic cost of gwei in the Ethereum network. Users can also decide to pay a *priority fee*. The priority fee is an additional amount of gwei a user can pay to get their transaction accepted faster. Transaction fees overall are calculated by gas cost X (base fee + priority fee). Let's imagine I want to send 2 ETH to another EOA. The gas cost per EOA-EOA transaction is 21,000. I need 21,000 gas units to compute. The base fee per unit of gas is currently 15 gwei. I decide to include a priority fee of 2 gwei. To find the overall transaction fee we need 21,000 gas cost X (15 gwei base fee + 2 gwei priority fee) = 357,000 gwei, which is 0.000357 ETH. In total, I will send 2.000357 ETH. Users can cap the maximum fee they are willing to pay and if the transaction costs less they will be refunded.[6] You can customise fees manually, but most Ethereum clients and wallet software calculate them automatically.

Transaction fees since the London Upgrade/ EIP-1559 have an interesting economic dynamic. The base fee is burnt and removed from circulation. The priority fee is paid to the users called validators we discuss in the next chapter. The idea is that in optimal conditions the burn rate of fees should exceed the emitted rewards that go to validators. This should decrease the overall supply of ETH and make it scarcer and therefore more valuable. This is known as the "ultra sound money" thesis.

Pulling this all together, we can see Ethereum transactions contain the following information:

From[7]:	The sending address.
To:	The receiving address.
Digital Signature:	A signature produced using the private key of the sender.
Nonce:	Shows how many transactions an account has made.
Value:	The ETH to be transferred.
Input Data:	Input data (message call); Initialise (contract creation).
Gas Limit:	Limit on gas.
Max Priority Fee:	Maximum priority fee you will pay.
Max Fee:	Maximum overall fee you will pay.

Ethereum Virtual Machine (EVM)

The Ethereum Virtual Machine (EVM) is responsible for executing transactions on Ethereum. Virtual machines are emulations of operating systems (OS). Imagine I am running the Windows operating system, but also want to run the Linux operating system on the same computer. One option is to install both by partitioning the hard drive. However, it is possible to use virtual machine software to emulate one operating system within another. Ethereum takes this virtual machine concept and tweaks it. Ethereum client developers create execution software clients, like Geth or Nethermind, that follow the same broad specification for executing transactions. When running this software, the EVM is emulated on the user's own hardware, like a Linux or Windows operating system. The task of the EVM is to process recent transactions to enable a transition to a new world state. The world state needs to change every 12 seconds. In each of these 12-second slots, one user, called a block proposer, is selected to propose the next state, in a data structure called a block.

The Ethereum Virtual Machine (EVM) is the Central Processing Unit (CPU) that coordinates the state transition (Figure 2.4). The *State Transition Function* refers to the various operations that move Ethereum from world state to world state. Straightforward EOA-EOA transactions are relatively easy to process and just need to pass a set of validity criteria such as having a valid signature, valid nonce and enough gas. However, transactions involving contract accounts are more complicated and require the full spectrum of the EVM.

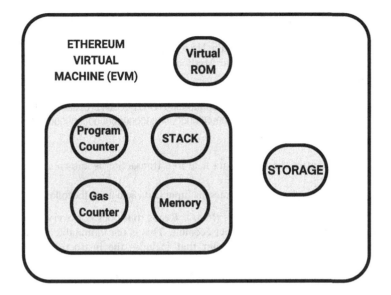

Figure 2.4 Ethereum Virtual machine (EVM).

Now let's imagine we have a Message Call transaction from an EOA to a contract account. For the EVM, the most important field is the Input Data field because it contains the function we want to call and the arguments we want to pass. In Solidity, the Input Data field follows the Application Binary Interface (ABI) format which is a standard that tells the smart contract how to interpret the Input Data field. A function is a command that the smart contract can execute and functions are identified in the ABI specification by the reference MethodID. The arguments are the changes requested, such as the specific address to send to or the value to be sent. For example, here's what a sample Input Data field would look like in the ABI format[8]:

Function: transfer(address to, uint256 value)

MethodID: 0xa9059cbb

[0]: 0000000000000000000000009f11260cb6427c20a019780d99d3a2d7 ffe9a253

[1]: 0000000000000000000000000000000000000000000000000000000000 2c8650c0

We see the transfer function from the contract's Code, which has its own MethodID, and the parameters involved, in this case, a recipient address and a value. The arguments are the specifics we want to be changed. The [0] is the recipient address and the [1] is the value.

In Bytecode we can see the MethodID leading and then the two arguments:

0xa9059cbb0000000000000000000000009f11260cb6427c20a019780d
99d3a2d7ffe9a253000000000000000000000000000000000000000000000
00000000000002c8650c0

The content of the Input Data field in a transaction is known as the *Call Data*.

The EVM interprets and executes the Input Data field using the following:

Virtual Read-Only Memory (ROM): Reads (but does not overwrite) the code of an involved contract account. This is the immutable Code contained in the contract account that includes the instructions for how the contract should operate.

Next, there is the machine state. This just means a temporary state for processing the transactions. It includes:

Program Counter: The program counter tracks what instructions from the contract code need to be processed next.

The Stack: The EVM uses a stack-based model for executing code. A stack is a Last-In-First-Out (LIFO) architecture. Opcodes are pushed to the top of the stack, executed and then popped out, to be replaced by the next.

EVM Memory: Temporary memory used within the machine state to track changes, that is disposed of once the transaction is processed.

Gas counter: Tracks the gas used. Reverts if no more gas is available and undoes the proposed state changes.

The results of the temporary machine state lead to changes in the permanent *Storage* of the contract account.

Storage: Changes are recorded permanently to reflect the new world state that emerges from the temporary machine state.

Once a transaction is processed, the EVM moves on to the next and the process begins all over again. The EVM will run through all transactions in sequence until none are left. It produces an execution payload. The execution payload is an output summary of the EVM's state transition function.

Smart Contract Case Studies

Smart contracts come in many forms, but we can illustrate them using two common formats: ERC-20 and ERC-721. But do keep in mind this does not mean they are the only contract types. It would be impossible to give all of them because Ethereum allows developers wide freedom to create contract applications. Notice my two examples start with ERC. This stands for Ethereum Request for Comment and is followed by an individual number. ERCs are application templates in Ethereum. They effectively outline a basic code standard for building something that others can borrow, tweak or expand. Having these broad templates is quite useful because pretty much anyone with a basic handle on Solidity (and sometimes those who don't) can launch new projects quickly, using the format as a basis. The two ERCs discussed here are for tokens, but ERCs do not have to relate to tokens.

ERC-20

The ERC-20 token standard creates fungible tokens. Fungible means the tokens will be "like-for-like." Any token I create will be equivalent to any other. This is the same as the money in your pocket, on your debit card or your phone. It does not matter if I buy milk with this particular dollar or euro. When a smart contract developer wants to create a fungible token in Solidity they can borrow the ERC-20 smart contract template. The code will outline important details about the token (name, total supply, etc.) and then what functions EOAs can call (transfer tokens, check balances, check name, check supply, etc.). Once the ERC-20 smart contract is deployed, this code becomes *the* Code in a smart contract account. This is the immutable Code the EVM pulls up in its Virtual Read-Only Memory (ROM) when it needs to know how the contract should run. The Storage in an ERC-20 is a database mapping EOA addresses to ERC-20 token balances within the contract account. Each time an EOA makes a Message Call with Input Data to the contract account, say to transfer tokens, the EVM will call the Code needed to change the Storage accordingly. Or, in plain English, a transaction from a user results in a change in token balances on the application. ERC-20 tokens are not just used as currencies. In later chapters, we'll see them used in clever ways, including as governance or voting tokens within blockchain communities.

ERC-721

The ERC-721 token standard is not dissimilar to the ERC-20 one. The core difference is that ERC-721 is designed to create Non-Fungible Tokens (NFTs). Unlike ERC-20 tokens, ERC-721 tokens are unique. Each ERC-721 token will have a unique identifier, usually a TokenID integer. It is possible the NFT will have associated metadata stored on-chain that uniquely identifies it even further, but most NFT contracts use a TokenURI, which links to metadata or the image associated with the

NFT stored externally. This can include external storage services like the Peer-to-Peer (P2P) InterPlanetary File System (IPFS) storage protocol or even Amazon Web Services (AWS). It is possible to create a contract for a single item, but usually, an NFT smart contract builds a collection of items that are a similar type, but with unique differences (e.g. 10,000 penguins, but each penguin has slightly different metadata traits and imagery). When a smart contract developer creates an NFT project, they will outline important details about the token (collection name, total supply, etc.) and then what functions EOAs can call (mint token, transfer tokens, check balances, check name, check supply, etc.). When an NFT project launches normally there is a function to mint the NFT. From then on, the NFTs can be sold and transferred between users, which the contract's Storage will map.

Decentralised Applications (dApps)

In an Ethereum context, a *Decentralised Applications (dApp)* refers to the smart contract plus the non-blockchain technologies it combines with to aid the user experience. With dApps, the contract account experience is mediated in some way. Most smart contract protocols have user-friendly front ends, in the form of traditional websites. For example, the Uniswap smart contract contains functions for swapping tokens. But to interact with the smart contract, Uniswap has created a website to make the process easier than interacting with a smart contract directly. Another example is the Bored Ape Yacht Club (BAYC) smart contract. The smart contract contains functions for minting and transferring an asset called a Bored Ape, but the images of the Bored Apes are not stored in the contract account, but instead use an external Peer-to-Peer (P2P) file-storage system. Since Storage can be expensive on Ethereum, it makes sense to logically extend the storage options for this particular dApp. The terms smart contract and dApp are commonly conflated, but I think there is value in understanding the distinction between the Ethereum native smart contract and the extension of that contract with non-blockchain services, making it a dApp.

Notes

1 Different Ethereum software clients store the "raw" database in different ways. For example, the Geth execution client will store it as a LevelDB database.
2 Ethereum uses Recursive Length Prefix (RLP) encoding to serialise information like an account's state. This technique takes the values for each field required and places them into a sequence together in binary form. For example, an EOA serialised would include a Nonce value and a Balance value. A contract serialised would have Nonce, Balance, Code and Storage. Ethereum

also uses this technique in other places, such as transactions. The Consensus Layer has its own version called Simple Serialize (SSZ).

3 Eight binary bits, which in hexadecimal are represented as two characters.

4 This is a don't overthink it moment. Contract accounts can't create transactions themselves, but must be triggered by EOAs into running their code. The one thing that is "like" a transaction that they can do is create contracts, but always an EOA must be the originating transaction prompt.

5 See Buterin V (2014) Launching the Ether Sale. Available at: https://blog. ethereum.org/2014/07/22/launching-the-ether-sale

6 Specifically, they can set the maximum priority fee they want to pay or an overall fee.

7 Technically not included in the transaction but easily inferable and shown by most block explorers.

8 This transaction is real and you can inspect it for yourself. I pulled it randomly: https://etherscan.io/tx/0xa47c82ba29272d82e1de8eec0e287b4584db0c505846a 36088e9832cf0b94ca3

3 Ethereum

The Consensus Layer (CL)

Since Ethereum is decentralised, there is no central authority that can decide on the current state of the world computer, known as the world state. The world state maps the addresses of user accounts called Externally-Owned Accounts (EOAs) and application accounts called contract accounts. To track the world state, Ethereum uses a *blockchain*, a secure record-keeping system that enables decentralised coordination among users who do not know or trust each other. Ethereum's blockchain is called the *Beacon Chain* and it has its own state, the *Beacon state*, that must also transition. In place of trusted third parties to make state transitions, blockchains have consensus mechanisms. A *consensus mechanism* is an incentivised protocol a blockchain uses to reach an agreement on a state of affairs. In Ethereum, the consensus mechanism is called Proof of Stake (PoS) or staking. Informally, staking involves validators putting up a stake of 32 ETH that grants them the right to participate in consensus. Every 12 seconds, in a slot, one validator is selected to propose a block representing the state transitions (world state, Beacon state). A committee of validators then votes/attests to the legitimacy of the block. Validators are rewarded for their participation in staking, but misbehaviour results in a loss of staked ETH. Validators are thereby incentivised both to honestly update Ethereum and disincentivised to dishonestly do so. When all is running well, every slot results in a transition that is captured in the block data structure. Once a block is finalised it becomes a part of the canonical history of the Ethereum blockchain and cannot be reverted.

Blocks and Blockchains

Let's start with a high-level view of blocks and blockchains and worry later about what precisely is included in Ethereum's blockchain. *Blocks* are data structures containing contextual information about a blockchain. A block is a snapshot of Ethereum at a point in time. A block can become the latest block in a chain of blocks, the blockchain (Figure 3.1).

DOI: 10.4324/9781003319603-3

A blockchain

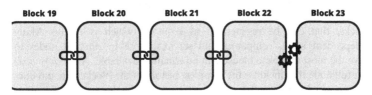

Figure 3.1 A blockchain.

Prior to this block's addition, a previous block had been accepted and had been the latest block. Prior to that block, another block was. The blocks stack on top of one another all the way back to Ethereum's original Genesis block 0 on July 30, 2015. Taken cumulatively, all the blocks are a permanent record of the activity that happened on Ethereum. Blockchains are distributed among all full node participants, rather than located in a single place. Remember, we don't have a central authority that can update the world computer, meaning we don't have a single entity that can add a block next. Instead, the consensus mechanism ensures all full nodes have the same history of the blockchain and enables the blockchain to be extended with a new block. Since there's no central authority, blockchains are also tamper-resistant, meaning nobody can unilaterally make changes to the history. Once a state of affairs is accepted it can't be reverted. Now, we'll see how people might attack a blockchain and try to change it, but when operating correctly, blockchains are immutable. Finally, blockchains are transparent, meaning all activity that happens on a blockchain is completely public. This is a side-effect of a decentralised network. Each full node needs a copy of the blockchain because we're all keeping an eye on one another, ensuring everyone is following the consensus mechanism protocol and not abusing the system.

This is a little hard to grasp at first, but there is no monolithic blockchain stored somewhere out there in the world. Instead, each individual full node in the Ethereum network keeps a copy of the blockchain. In Ethereum, there are three main types of nodes: full, archival and light. We call a user running a full node a node operator. A full node is composed of a software execution client and a consensus client. Execution client options include Geth, Nethermind, Besu and Erigon. Consensus client options include Prysm, Teku, Lighthouse, Nimbus and Lodestar. The use of multiple options is known as *client diversity* and it is designed to ensure that any issue found in one client does not impact the entire network. A full node can independently verify transactions, the world state and the blockchain. A full node can achieve this because they have a "complete" copy of the blockchain. I say "complete" because most full node software prunes the blockchain. With pruning, a certain depth of blocks is kept but only snapshots of historical blocks, that can be regenerated as required (which is rarely). Many independent users, companies and services chose to run full nodes to have the most complete blockchain information available. An *archive node* is a full node that includes the complete history of the blockchain and does not prune. Archive nodes can be quite demanding in terms of storage resources and are really only for the purists. Finally, at the other end of the spectrum, are *light nodes* (sometimes called light clients) which depend on full nodes for information about the blockchain. 'There is one more entity, known as a validator, who is responsible for updating the blockchain through the staking consensus mechanism.'

Proof of Stake (PoS) or Staking

For approximately seven years (2015–2022), Ethereum used the same Proof of Work (PoW) or mining consensus mechanism as Bitcoin, but with some variations.[1] Mining sees users compete to update a blockchain by engaging in a competitive computational race to find a puzzle solution. This design led to an unforeseen arms race that made mining inaccessible to everyday users and turned it into a specialist and even industrial enterprise. This is because mining requires the use of custom machines known as Application Specific Integrated Circuits (ASICs). Cumulatively, ASICs make heavy energy demands and Bitcoin has earned a reputation in the mainstream as environmentally problematic. However, I would encourage readers to research mining themselves and make up their own minds, especially as many in the Bitcoin community have worked hard to address this problem. Regardless, staking is preferred by the Ethereum community because (a) the environmental impact is much lower and (b) there are no custom machines, making participation in consensus much easier. Ethereum transitioned to staking from mining in September 2022 in an event known as The Merge, reducing energy consumption by an eye-watering 99.95%. The Merge was a major under-taking that required a live switch from mining to staking and, to the immense credit of the developers, it went without a hitch.

Validators

To understand staking we'll approach it from the perspective of stakers. When we broadly talk about the individuals involved in staking we call them stakers. For example, superphiz.eth is a well-known staker in the Ethereum community. Stakers participate in the consensus mechanism by running validators. A *validator* is an account with 32 ETH deposited to the deposit contract as collateral (the stake). To become a validator, a staker needs to be a full-node operator (execution, consensus) and then briefly uses a *validator client* to opt-in to staking. The *deposit contract* is a contract account list of participating validators. There is a validator queue to ensure the network is not overloaded. The 32 ETH stake is important because it ensures sybil resistance. In a blockchain context, we don't want malicious entities to be able to spin up no-cost validating nodes, sybils. Real ETH has to be put at stake by an attacker and potentially lost due to Ethereum's self-defence mechanisms.

Once a validator is no longer in the queue they join the *validator set*. As part of the set, a validator's job is to decide on the immediate head of the blockchain and to finalise blocks. The first task, the head of the blockchain, is decided using a Latest Message Driven Greedy Heaviest-Observed Sub-Tree (LMD GHOST) vote. This fulfils the property of liveness, meaning blocks are added quickly. The second task, to finalise blocks, is decided using a Casper the Friendly Finality Gadget (Casper-FFG) vote. The Casper-FFG vote has two parts (justification and finalisation) that lead to the finalisation of a historical point in the blockchain. This fulfils the property of finality, where we can be assured that blocks up to a certain point are permanent. This means there are three votes overall: head of the chain, justification and finalisation. When discussed as a unit, LMD GHOST and Casper-FFG combine to become Gasper.

Validators work within a timeframe split up into slots and epochs. The LMD GHOST vote happens in a slot and the Casper-FFG vote happens across epochs (Figure 3.2).

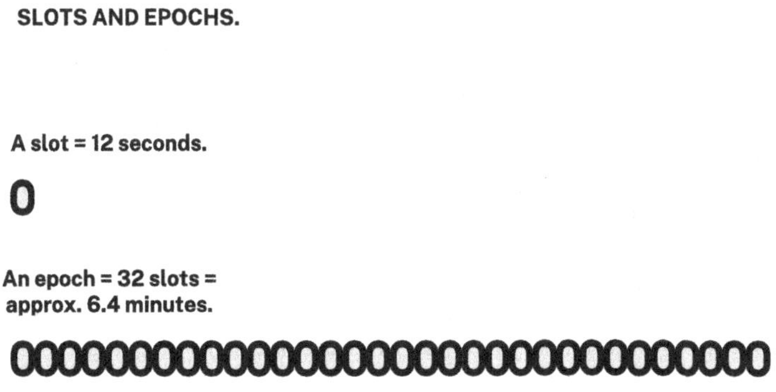

SLOTS AND EPOCHS.

A slot = 12 seconds.

O

An epoch = 32 slots = approx. 6.4 minutes.

OOOOOOOOOOOOOOOOOOOOOOOOOOOOOOOO

Figure 3.2 Slots and an epoch.

Slot: 12 seconds.

Epoch: 32 slots long or approximately 6.4 minutes.

Slots and LMD GHOST

Let's focus on slots first. A *slot* is a 12-second window where a block can be proposed as the latest head of the blockchain. In every slot, a block proposer is randomly selected as the leader. Only *one* validator is assigned as the block proposer for a slot. Block proposers are chosen in advance using a pseudo-random algorithm called RANDAO. It is possible for a slot to be empty if the block proposer does not propose a block (e.g. they are offline), but generally speaking, most slots are filled. To be chosen to propose a block is a relatively uncommon event. The block proposer's job is fourfold. First, they look back at the last slot and find the previous block with the most attestations, the "heaviest" block. Second, they construct a new Beacon block with contextual information – such as entering and exiting validators, penalties for misbehaving validators, etc. – that transitions Ethereum to a new Beacon state. Third, in their execution client, they transition the world state by gathering transactions from the mempool, executing them in the EVM, and producing the execution payload, in the form of an execution block. Fourth, they sign the block and then present it to the validators to attest to. However, they don't present it to the entire validator set.

We have one block proposer, but what are the other validators doing during the slot? The majority of the time, validators are involved in attestation. *Attestations* are analogous to votes in the staking context and are weighted according to a validator's balance (more on this later). The first attestation is the LMD GHOST vote to the latest proposed block at the head of the blockchain. This vote pertains to a specific slot the validator has been assigned to, as part of a committee (also chosen using RANDAO). *Committees* are groups of attesting validators assigned to validate a proposed block in a slot. Committees are formed from the set of validators staking in the deposit contract. In an epoch, validators are randomly distributed into committees for one of the 32 slots. For example, as I was writing this there were approximately 703,000 active validators. These were distributed into epoch 219,146. Which means each slot would have approximately 22,000 committee members. If we look at one of the slots in this epoch, slot 7,012,687, we find there were 21,908 attesting validators. The validators in the slot's committee sign off on the block proposed by the block proposer. In effect, they are attesting to the validity of the proposed transition. The block proposer in the next slot will then build on this block since it has the most attestations.

LMD GHOST

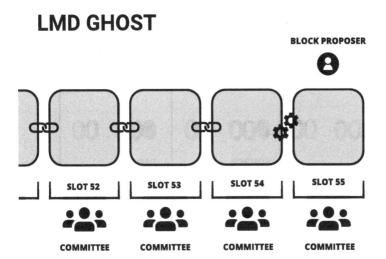

Figure 3.3 LMD GHOST.

If the slot is empty, perhaps because the assigned block proposer is offline, then the committee will vote for the previous block as remaining at the latest. There also exists the *sync committee*, which is a selection of validators who are serving light clients. Participation in a sync committee is fairly rare (Figure 3.3).

Epochs and Casper-FFG

The second attestation a validator makes, the Casper-FFG vote, is more general and really is two votes. With *Casper-FFG*, validators attest to two checkpoints. *Checkpoints* are the first filled slots at the start of an epoch. If there is no block in this slot then the prior block becomes the checkpoint. The first checkpoint is the *target* and refers to the checkpoint at the start of the current epoch. The second checkpoint is the *source* and refers to the checkpoint in the epoch prior. If a 2/3 supermajority votes on the target checkpoint then it becomes justified. If the source, the justified target in the prior epoch, attracts a 2/3 supermajority it becomes finalised. Once blocks are finalised they are considered a permanent part of the Ethereum blockchain and cannot be reverted. I detail the importance of the 2/3 supermajority in the section on malicious forks and attacks, but right now let's stick with the scenario where the majority of validators are honest (Figure 3.4).

CASPER-FFG

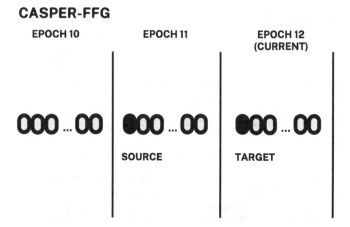

Figure 3.4 Casper-FFG.

Aggregation

To improve the efficiency of attestations, validators use the Boneh–Lynn–Shacham Digital Signature (BLS) digital signature scheme. It is similar to the ECDSA signature scheme we encountered for Externally-Owned Accounts (EOA). However, BLS signatures have an interesting property, they can be verified in aggregate almost as quickly as individual signatures can. To really speed matters up, committees are themselves subdivided into 64 subnets. Within each subnet, a validator is chosen as the aggregator. The aggregator gathers all the signed attestations that are in agreement about the block, target and source and presents them as a single aggregated signature to the block proposer. The block proposer will include the aggregated signature from the subnets in the Beacon block.

Rewards and Penalties

What does our validator get for their participation in staking? Staking is an incentivised protocol. We want as many people as possible to be involved in the process to ensure wide decentralisation. But we also want some mechanisms that punish bad behaviour. This is accomplished using a rewards and penalties system.

Block proposal: Proposing a block. Includes priority fees and MEV.
Attestations: Attesting to the block, to the checkpoints.
Sync committee: Participation in a sync committee.
Slashing reward: Reporting malicious behaviour.

Block proposal can be valuable because it includes any priority fees and any Maximum Extractable Value (MEV) (later topic), but it's not common. However, all validators attest in every epoch and receive the smaller attestation reward for it. A small boost occurs for validators that perform consistently. Participating in a sync committee for light nodes or slashing rewards is relatively rare.

Now let's turn to the penalties system. The below penalties are often the result of your validator going offline. The penalties are relatively small if they happen occasionally.

Missed Proposal:	No penalty.
Missed Attestation:	Failure to attest.
Missed Committee:	Failure to participate in sync committee.

Alongside the above, validators can be punished for malicious behaviour. The punishment here is more serious and known as slashing. *Slashing* is the penalty for a validator engaging in equivocation, i.e. proposing or attesting in a conflicting manner. With LMD GHOST, block proposers can be slashed if they propose two or more blocks. Validators can be slashed if they attest to two blocks as the head of the chain. With Casper-FFG, validators can be slashed if they attest to more than one target checkpoint. Equivocation is met immediately with a slashing of 1/32 of their ETH (maximum penalty is 1 ETH) and the validator then enters an exit period of 36 days. Halfway through the exiting process, on day 18, a correlation penalty is imposed that is relative to the amount of slashed ETH within the network. If few validators were slashed the correlation penalty would be small, but if a large number were slashed it could end up high, possibly even a validator's entire stake.

Beacon Block

You can likely survive not knowing what's really included in a block, but I know some of you are gluttons for punishment. Ethereum's "main" block is the Beacon block. It includes all the information related to the consensus mechanism, such as the current slot, who the block proposer is, what the previous block was, who has been slashed, any new validators from the deposit contract, and the signature, among others. It also includes all the attestations gathered during the slot from the validator committee. The attestations bless the block as legitimate and the next block proposer will look to this block as the heaviest, meaning it has the most attestations, and will then extend their own fresh block on top of it. I said the Beacon block is the "main block" and that is because it includes the execution payload as an

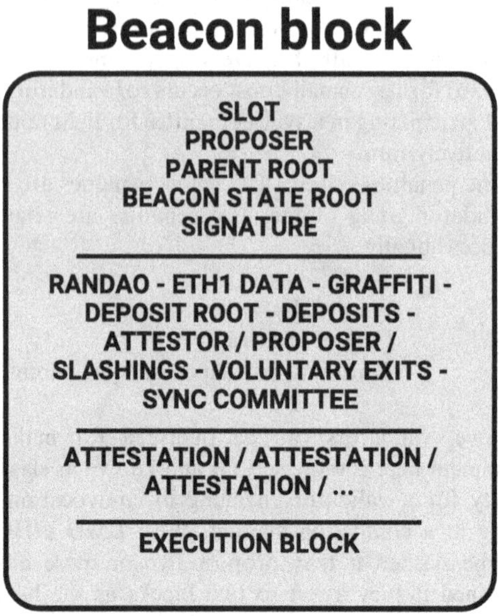

Beacon block

**SLOT
PROPOSER
PARENT ROOT
BEACON STATE ROOT
SIGNATURE**

**RANDAO - ETH1 DATA - GRAFFITI -
DEPOSIT ROOT - DEPOSITS -
ATTESTOR / PROPOSER /
SLASHINGS - VOLUNTARY EXITS -
SYNC COMMITTEE**

**ATTESTATION / ATTESTATION /
ATTESTATION / ...**

EXECUTION BLOCK

Figure 3.5 Beacon block.

execution block nested within itself. When a block proposer proposes a block, they send transactions to the execution client to produce an execution payload, which is formatted into an execution block.[2] The execution block is then transmitted to the consensus client and incorporated into the Beacon block (Figure 3.5).

You'll also notice certain fields in the block are Roots. These are cryptographic hashes. They are produced using hash functions, which take data of arbitrary size and output fixed-length outputs. Using hash functions we can give data, even large amounts, a completely unique identifier. Ethereum calls these hashes Roots and uses them to make large amounts of data efficiently and securely verifiable. These Roots are built from hashes of sub-items contained in the states or lists they summarise. For example, the State Root in the execution block is a summary of each sub-item in the world state: EOAs, contract accounts and contract account Storage. They are all given hash identities and then stored in what's called a Merkle Patricia Tree. The summary Root sits at the stop and then all the sub-items branch off from it. We can see in the Beacon block Transactions, Receipts and Withdrawals are also summarised as hash Roots, which makes sense since they are all large amounts of data we might need to securely and efficiently verify.

Why are hash Roots useful? When a block proposer proposes a new block we can see they reference the Parent Root of the previous block, which is its hash summary. When attesting to blocks, validators expect to see the same Parent Root their own copy of the blockchain has. If there is a different Parent Root, it tells us immediately that something has been changed in the block. The same is true for the State Root of the world state. The State Root captures all the changes to the world state that happened during the state transition function. When a block proposer creates a State Root in their execution client, they report it to the validators. Validators re-execute the transactions in order to see whether they arrive at the same State Root. In other words, Roots are an efficient and secure technique to establish we're working with the same block/blockchain and to identify any kind of underhanded changes. Generally speaking, this is true of all the information in a block. You don't need to grasp all the details of what exactly is included in a block, but just the core concept that blocks capture all the information relevant to enable the execution and consensus layers to transition their states. As you get more advanced you might return and investigate the block structure, perhaps by examining real blocks on a block explorer such as Etherscan (Figure 3.6).

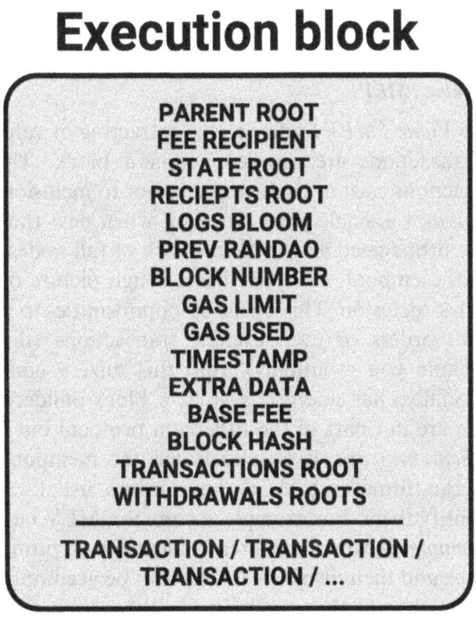

Execution block

PARENT ROOT
FEE RECIPIENT
STATE ROOT
RECIEPTS ROOT
LOGS BLOOM
PREV RANDAO
BLOCK NUMBER
GAS LIMIT
GAS USED
TIMESTAMP
EXTRA DATA
BASE FEE
BLOCK HASH
TRANSACTIONS ROOT
WITHDRAWALS ROOTS

TRANSACTION / TRANSACTION / TRANSACTION / ...

Figure 3.6 Execution block.

Advanced Staking Topics

Staking Pools

Staking pools combine smaller amounts of ETH to create shared validators. Pools are not native to the Ethereum protocol, but instead emerged as a service to address the desire of smaller ETH holders to participate in staking. There are two main types of staking pools. Centralised staking pools are operated by centralised exchanges. Users who have deposited ETH on an exchange can stake their ETH and the exchange will then pool the ETH to create validators, distributing the rewards to the user. Decentralised pools are smart contract protocols. Users interact with the staking pools' smart contract by depositing ETH and receiving a Liquid Staking Derivative (LSD) token in return. The LSD token represents their stake plus any accumulated rewards. Users can unstake by swapping back the LSD token for the original ETH deposit and any staking rewards accumulated. Staking pools are a useful tool in allowing users without 32 ETH to participate in staking, but there is an associated problem. Most users of staking pools tend to use a small number of centralised (e.g. Binance) and decentralised staking pools (Lido, Rocket Pool) and this gives those pools a large percentage of the overall staking distribution. In other words, staking pools can cause centralisation of the staking consensus mechanism.

Maximum Extractable Value (MEV)

Maximum Extractable Value (MEV) refers to the extracting of value by manipulating how transactions are ordered within a block. This is possible because transactions exist in the mempool prior to inclusion on-chain. The mempool is not a single place. Instead, when new transactions are sent, they are propagated across the network of full nodes that add them to their local mempool. Everyone has a rough picture of the *potential* transactions for inclusion. This opens up opportunities to place transactions in certain orders or even exclude transactions (though someone else will include you eventually). Into this mix, a complex ecosystem of MEV specialists has emerged: searchers, block builders and relayers. These entities are not part of the Ethereum protocol but have built up around it. *Searchers* are users who watch the mempool for transactions that they can format into MEV opportunities, usually using automated bots to identify them. For example, a common MEV tactic is frontrunning. *Frontrunning* is when a searcher identifies a profitable trade from another user and then displaces it. This can be accomplished by copying the transaction and then swapping in the searcher's own details, but with a higher gas fee.

Around MEV, an ecosystem of actors has emerged around a middleware technology called MEV-Boost. While block proposers propose blocks and can construct their own payloads, in practice this is often outsourced to entities called block builders. Technically, the Ethereum protocol has always intended to separate block proposals from block building, but it proved too complex to implement during The Merge. Eventually, Proposer-Builder Separation (PBS) will be enshrined into the protocol, but for now it is a semi-formal distinction. *Block builders* use the mempool to build an execution payload, but they also include the optimised MEV transactions from searchers. The built block will include a payment to the block proposer. Another party, called a relay or relayer, passes the block builder blocks to proposers, who select the most profitable one for them.

Now, there is one very important recent story for understanding how blocks are built in the era of MEV and OFAC compliance. In 2022, the U.S. Department of the Treasury's Office of Foreign Assets Control (OFAC) sanctioned the Tornado Cash mixing protocol and a set of addresses associated with it. Tornado Cash is a privacy tool that allows users to anonymise their ETH but has become linked with money laundering. Since Ethereum is a decentralised protocol, there is no central authority that can enforce OFAC compliance. It then becomes a choice of actors within the network whether they wish to comply or not. In particular, the decision impacts relayers since relayers are the ones commonly passing on blocks to block proposers. Some relayers choose to censor Tornado Cash and some don't. This means your transaction will go through, but possibly at a delay, depending on which relayer is involved.

Blockchain Forks

Forks can be good or bad depending on the context. Positively, forking is how new upgrades are introduced to a blockchain protocol. Negatively, if a blockchain is forking unintentionally then it's a problem.

Let's examine the main types of forks:

Temporary chain split: Two or more blocks are temporarily seen as the head of the blockchain. These occurrences are typically resolved quickly as nodes converge on one version of the chain over the other. In Ethereum, if two or more blocks are seen by the network, then the LMD GHOST fork choice rule will select the one with the most attestations.

Soft fork: New changes to the protocol are introduced, but are backwards compatible. Full nodes can choose to run older software clients without the new changes. In Ethereum, this is not a common method, but in Bitcoin, it is the standard.

Hard fork: New changes to the protocol are introduced, but are not backwards compatible. The changes are significant enough that they change how the protocol works. This means the older full-node client software won't be able to process or accept new blocks, rendering them unable to participate in the network. Ethereum is a protocol that routinely introduces major changes and therefore requires hard forks. You may hear Bitcoiners raise this as an issue, but it is not commonly understood as one within Ethereum culture.

Contentious Hard Fork: It is also possible for users to reject hard forks and continue to follow the non-forked version of the blockchain. In this instance, the two groups, those who follow the hard fork and those who don't, no longer follow the same blockchain. This happened to Ethereum in 2016 when a major project called The DAO suffered an exploit. The issue was resolved by a hard fork. The majority continued to follow the hard forked chain, the Ethereum we have today, and a minority continued to follow the old non-hard forked chain, renamed as Ethereum Classic. Conversely, you can perform a contentious hard fork in the other direction. A community could be split over the future of the protocol. To settle the dispute, one side can create a version of the protocol through a hard fork and effectively branch off in their own direction. In 2017, a minority subculture within Bitcoin created a hard fork called Bitcoin Cash that changed the protocol rules of the original Bitcoin. However, the majority culture remained with the non-hard forked version, which is the Bitcoin we have today.

Malicious hard fork: A malicious hard fork is where a single entity or colluding cohort gains majority control of the consensus mechanism. In these scenarios, the attacker will need a substantial percentage of staked ETH. In a "reorg" attack, the malicious actor could displace blocks attested as the head of the blockchain. This is achieved by intentionally withholding attestations in a slot and then attesting twice in the next slot to make their desired block the one with the most attestations, the heaviest. This requires controlling 34% of staked ETH. In a finality delay attack, a malicious attacker with 34% staked ETH is the block proposer for the first slot in an epoch. The attacker delays slightly. To the other validators, the slot would appear empty and they attest to the previous block as the target. We will then have two conflicting targets, which prevents finalisation. However, this attack would eventually incur the *inactivity leak* penalty that re-asserts the honest supermajority over time. It kicks in after four epochs without finalisation. If 1/3 of staked ETH held by validators is either inactive (e.g. offline) or malicious, they are slashed until the honest validators are returned to a 2/3 supermajority, allowing finalisation to occur. An attacker with 66% of ETH would effectively control the consensus mechanism since they form a 2/3 supermajority. In this scenario, the protocol is not in a position to help and the response needs to come from Ethereum's social layer, most likely through a hard fork. Broadly speaking, these attacks are mitigated by the sheer amount of staked ETH needed to perform them. At the time of writing, 23,487,763 ETH are staked in the deposit contract and when you are reading this it will almost certainly be much more.

What Is Ethereum, Really?

This is the most difficult chapter. From here on out it's more or less plain sailing. But let's summarise what we know so far. Ethereum is a world computer. This computer has a Central Processing (CPU) called the Ethereum Virtual Machine (EVM). The EVM transitions from world state to world state every 12 seconds. The transitions are set in motion by Externally-Owned Accounts (EOAs) that either send transactions to one another, create new contract accounts or call functions in contract accounts. A block proposer is chosen in a slot to propose a new block. The proposer constructs a Beacon block that looks back at the last block and grabs the one with the most attestations as its parent. It fills in important new information about deposits, slashings, withdrawals, etc. The proposer also needs to transition the world state. The world state is like the Random Access Memory (RAM) on your computer. It's all the "live" content reflecting user activity. The proposer processes transactions in their execution client's EVM and outputs the execution payload, with the new world state. We bundle this into an execution block and nest it in the Beacon block. We then communicate it to the validators assigned to our slot's committee within an epoch. The validators check the Beacon block's information is legitimate and then re-execute the payload to arrive at the world state. If everything checks out they attest to the block. The attestations are aggregated and included as a single signature. After 12 seconds, the block slots in, waiting to be picked up by the next block proposer as the heaviest block, the head of the blockchain. Validators also attested to the target and the source checkpoints and finalised a past block as part of the permanent history of the blockchain. The blockchain, we can now see, is like our computer's hard drive, the deep storage. The Ethereum world computer is therefore the CPU (EVM) plus the RAM (world state) plus the hard drive (blockchain).

Notes

1 The Ethereum version was known as Ethash. Probably its most distinguishing feature was its ASIC-resistant design, meaning it was easier for everyday users to mine using Graphics Processing Units (GPUs) at home. ASICs are custom mining machines that can be quite expensive.
2 I want to highlight here the Gas Limit found in the execution block. Ethereum blocks are measured by their *Gas Limit* (distinct, confusingly, from the Gas Limit a user places on a transaction). Ethereum is a Turing Complete

computer, meaning developers can create loops and conditionals. This allows them versatility in creating smart contracts, but it contains a hidden problem, the halting problem. The halting problem refers to the fact that a malicious developer could create a smart contract that endlessly loops. To address this, blocks have a *Gas Limit* to cap the computation that can occur within a block. The Gas Limit is dynamic but has a target size of 15 million gas. If there is demand this can increase up to 30 million gas, but when this happens the base fee increases. The increase is designed to return the Gas Limit back to the target size of 15 million gas.

4 Ethereum Governance and Culture

Blockchain governance refers to the coordination mechanisms that allow blockchain stakeholders to make legitimate decisions. Blockchain governance is traditionally split up into two broad areas: on-chain governance and off-chain governance. In the context of Ethereum, on-chain governance relates to the Ethereum protocol. The on-chain protocol rules stipulate how Ethereum the technology should work, such as what transactions are acceptable, how a block is added or how validators are rewarded. Off-chain governance refers to the management and maintenance of the Ethereum protocol. Off-chain governance consists of open-source procedures – developer and researcher meetings, GitHub repositories and Ethereum Improvement Proposals (EIPs) – where users can propose changes to the Ethereum protocol and implement them.

Blockchain culture is the social, cultural or political values shared by a blockchain community. Blockchains record novel experiments in money, organisation, finance, and art that reflect the cultural interests of their communities. Ethereum's culture is multifaceted and dynamic but builds on a core set of values. The first value is especially important in Ethereum and almost every other blockchain community: political decentralisation. Political decentralisation means authority is spread among all participating members, rather than concentrated. Political decentralisation is supported by the technical decentralisation of how Ethereum is structured. Just slightly below decentralisation, we find more values important to Ethereans: permissionlessness (no permission required to use Ethereum); censorship resistance (nobody can censor you on Ethereum) and credible neutrality (Ethereum's operations should be fair to everyone). Governance and culture are tightly interrelated because governance is supposed to reflect the values of the culture.

Ethereum Governance

Satoshi Nakamoto, the inventor of Bitcoin, released Bitcoin as open-source software. *Open-source* development means volunteers work

DOI: 10.4324/9781003319603-4

collaboratively to make non-proprietary software where the code is freely available for users to inspect and even to copy and build upon. Ethereum adopts this model of open-source development wholesale. This model applies to many projects built on Ethereum as well. Ethereum's main codebases are hosted on the open-source development platform GitHub. The Ethereum GitHub contains various code repositories the community recognises as essential or core to Ethereum. These are as follows:

Official Go implementation of the Ethereum protocol: there is no single implementation of the Ethereum software, but instead numerous options in different programming languages. However, the main Ethereum repository includes the Go software client known as Geth. Prior to Ethereum's launch, three different implementations were focused on: C++ (Gavin Wood), Go (Jeffrey Wilcke) and Python (Vitalik Buterin). In a somewhat competitive spirit, the first two competed to be the template implementation and Buterin's Python implementation was seen as more suited to research. In the end, Wilcke's Go version worked best as a template.

Ethereum Improvement Proposals (EIPs): EIPs are the governance mechanism for major changes to the Ethereum protocol. More on these in a moment.

Solidity: created by Gavin Wood and Christian Reitwiessner, Solidity is a high-level programming language for writing smart contracts. Smart contracts can be written in other languages, such as Vyper, but Solidity dominates the landscape.

Remix: an Integrated Developer Environment (IDE) and compiler for Solidity that is accessible within your browser.

Ethereum.org website: this is the Ethereum homepage and consists of extensive and user-friendly information about all facets of Ethereum. It is maintained as an open-source effort with a small support staff. It is probably one of the most accessible means for readers of this book to become actively involved in Ethereum. Just go to their Discord and ask where they need help.

The development process for GitHub *in general* is as follows. This process is used in all the above cases, but expect nuance once you get involved:

Issues: users publicly suggest changes, whether bug fixes or improvements. Discussion about the Issues might happen.

Pull Requests: developers, whether from the public or the project team involved, propose conceptual or code solutions to Issues. Discussion about the Pull Request might happen. If the PR generates interest and broad support, it will pass some checks and then be merged into the next release (whether a new version of Geth or a new page for ethereum.org). Each repository will have members, usually from the project team, that can merge code, called having *commit access*. If the PR is controversial, it might cause a community rift.

We need to pay special attention to the Official Go implementation of the Ethereum protocol which is implemented in a software client called Geth. The development process for Ethereum software clients is used for changes that relate to the specific client. They don't relate to the Ethereum protocol itself. These changes must be compatible with the Ethereum protocol. For example, you can't request the Geth team to merge code that uses the mining consensus mechanism, because Ethereum now uses the staking mechanism. This proposal would mean Geth could not work with Ethereum. The same holds for the other software clients. Instead, any Issues and Pull Requests will usually concern bugs or improvements that impact the specific software client and how it implements the Ethereum protocol.

What about when someone proposes a change to the Ethereum protocol rather than a specific software client? This kind of suggestion has its own special process: Ethereum Improvement Proposals (EIPs). EIPs have their own repository on the Ethereum GitHub. EIPs follow a template where the proposer, known as the champion, will provide the rationale and the proposed technical specification. These changes can relate to various parts of Ethereum. The most well-known are Core EIPs which are upgrades or improvements requiring a fork, usually a hard fork in Ethereum (discussed in Chapter 3). EIPs are extensively discussed. A subset of EIPs, called Ethereum Request for Comments (ERC), is related to standards for smart contracts and dApps, and at the time of writing, there is a discussion to separate ERCs from EIPs, rendering ERCs their own category.

A famous Core EIP is EIP-1559 which proposed gas fees be burnt rather than sent to stakers. This was a change to the Ethereum protocol and not just a client team. It therefore needed to garner support from all quarters. This meant as close to all the stakeholders possible in the Ethereum ecosystem had to support it before it went live in 2021. Remember, Ethereum is politically decentralised to a strong degree so there is no centralised entity that can decide on behalf of everyone else. Decision-making is spread among many blockchain stakeholders. *Blockchain stakeholders* are groups with a stake or interest, whether financial or cultural, in a blockchain implementation. Ethereum's stakeholders in no particular order are as follows:

Ethereum users: the everyday Ethereum end user. Just your Average Joe and Jane sending USDC or joining a DAO or buying an NFT.

Ethereum media: specialist media and influencers such as podcasts or YouTube shows e.g. *The Daily Gwei* or the *Bankless Podcast*.

Ethereum project teams: the various decentralised applications (dApps) teams that are building on the Ethereum blockchain.

Ethereum developers: open-source developers and researchers who work on Ethereum client software or the protocol. This also includes protocol support members and coordinators.

Ethereum stakers: users who help to secure Ethereum's blockchain.

Ethereum Foundation (EF): a non-profit providing support for conferences (e.g. Devcon), developer meetings, the ethereum.org website and offering grants.

An EIP proposal might not garner any interest, but every so often some will. When this happens, the EIP will most likely be picked up by the Ethereum developers and researchers.

The developers congregate on the Ethereum's Magician forum and the Ethereum R&D Discord (Research and Development). In these hubs, developers and researchers meet to coordinate and discuss issues, including representatives from the various client software teams. Every week or so there is a meeting called AllCoreDevs where the most important issues around the Ethereum protocol are discussed. There are several smaller, more niche discussion meetings as well.

Ethereum's logistics are generally handled by the Ethereum Foundation (EF), the non-profit created at the launch of Ethereum. It has other roles too, such as organising and hosting Ethereum conferences (e.g. Devcon) and providing grants for Ethereum research (e.g. the Ecosystem Support Program). However, its everyday role is providing several dedicated full-time staff who work on Ethereum, which includes developers and researchers, but also protocol support members. For example, the Ethereum Cat Herders is a collective that helps with logistics, but also cleans up EIPs. The Cat Herders include EF and non-EF staff. The Protocol Guild, with EF and non-EF members, manages a smart contract that rewards open-source developers of Ethereum. Somewhat amusingly, the logistical role of the Ethereum Foundation is often conflated with centralised control of Ethereum, which must be a surprise to those tasked with herding the various cats across numerous stakeholders in the ecosystem, especially those who must get all the client teams in one place each week.

There is no exact science as to how an EIP garners support. Over time it gains support from developers and researchers and quite often it will be raked over the coals for any potential issues it might cause. EIPs will then attract people to contribute toward any further research, testing, or coding required. News about this EIP will begin to filter out to the other stakeholders. Ethereum validators or project teams might express their own support or concerns. Ethereum media and users might start to discuss it among themselves. An EIP that manages to gain a positive response from the various Ethereum stakeholders – but especially the developers and researchers in the AllCoreDevs call – reaches a rough consensus that the EIP should be implemented. In open-source development culture, there is rarely complete consensus, but instead, a rough consensus is reached across the many distributed parties. Again, there's no perfect science here, but usually you can recognise rough consensus by the disappearance of concerns, critiques or controversies. Once accepted, the EIP will be included in the next Ethereum upgrade and become part of the general developer and researcher discussion about how to coordinate and integrate the EIP in the various software clients in preparation for the upgrade. EIP upgrades are often bundled together these days. In Ethereum, upgrades are introduced through hard forks. This means the upgrade is not backwards compatible and full nodes will need to update their software clients in order to follow the Ethereum blockchain.

Governing a blockchain like Ethereum is the responsibility of the community collectively and each stakeholder in the wider community has *some* influence, albeit sometimes small. The optimal governance state, central to the belief systems behind almost all blockchain communities, is decentralisation. The rationale, at least at this abstract level, is to replace centralised governance with decentralised governance. Centralised institutions, companies, organisations and governments are seen as inherently corrupted or corruptible. However, the desire to implement decentralised alternatives does not always go to plan and centralisation tends to reassert itself, even in the most mindful of blockchain communities. The reality of decentralisation is more like a dance, where centralised power is disrupted by decentralisation, new forms of centralisation appear and renewed efforts at decentralisation occur in acts of re-decentralisation. To be a good citizen in Ethereum is to keep an eye on what you believe might be centralised points of influence and to raise concerns and disrupt centralisation where you find it. Generally speaking, Ethereum governance is highly decentralised, but with some light centralisation around logistics.

Ethereum Culture

Ethereum has no dominant culture and Ethereans can on principle be drawn from any culture, in the spirit of an open permissionless protocol. Despite this, there are recognisably popular subcultures within Ethereum and we can learn a lot about the protocol by looking at who is attracted to it. Since culture is dynamic, some of these subcultures will continue to flourish on Ethereum and others might dissipate.

Cypherpunk: many of Ethereum's influential developers and researchers are influenced by cypherpunk ideals. Cypherpunk was one of the foundational subcultures in Bitcoin and it carried over into parts of the Ethereum world. A cypherpunk is committed to open-source development and a certain DIY or punk attitude. Cypherpunks believe the best way to solve problems is to create the solution yourself and then disseminate the results freely, even allowing others to copy and build upon them. Cypherpunks usually stress an apolitical position regarding what they build should be used for. In Ethereum's case, the cypherpunks build the infrastructure and tools, but are hands-off about how they are used, taking a neutral stance. Historically, cypherpunk had an explicit emphasis on privacy, but in Ethereum, it is not always prioritised, albeit this seems to be changing. A neo-cypherpunk movement called lunarpunk has also emerged to advocate for placing privacy back front and centre. You can find cypherpunks on Ethereum's Magician forum, the Ethereum R&D Discord (Research and Development) or by attending events like ETHDenver.

Regens: many influential voices within Ethereum are committed to a regen or regenerative approach to building technology. Rooted in Vitalik Buterin's interest in politics and social science, many regens engage in governance experiments designed to reinvigorate, improve, or even replace contemporary institutions. This subculture is characterised by its experimental nature and interest in public goods, engaging in experiments such as Quadratic Funding (QF), Soulbound Tokens (SBT) and retroactive public goods funding. Regens are less focused on financial applications and more drawn to the idea of building a new decentralised Web, sometimes called Web3. Regens usually, but not always, tend to hold more progressive forms of politics and are associated with an aesthetic called solarpunk. You can find regens in public goods communities like Gitcoin or Optimism and at ETHBarcelona.

Degens: within Ethereum, there exists a contingent of users driven purely by speculation and wealth accumulation at all costs, the degens (degenerates). Degens are financial nihilists who focus on current trends and hype to strike it lucky and escape the rat race of contemporary neoliberal capitalism. Degens will often take extraordinary risks, but in an ironic, almost detached way. Degens usually, but not always, tend to hold more provocative political views and are associated with a more anime-type aesthetic. You can find degens in and around newly launched Decentralised Finance (DeFi) or Non-Fungible Token (NFT) launches or by attending conferences like NYC.NFT.

5 Decentralised Autonomous Organisations (DAOs)

Decentralised Autonomous Organisations (DAOs) are communities that self-organise using blockchain technology. DAOs have no particular use case and can be built for any purpose. DAOs typically (but not always) contain three components. *First*, DAOs use a suite of governance technologies to manage their affairs. This normally involves a governance token and then custom DAO voting tools such as Snapshot or Governor, which we'll discuss later. Since the votes are settled on the Ethereum blockchain, it too can be considered part of the governance technologies. *Second*, there is a social component in the form of online spaces to gather and discuss issues, such as Discord servers, Telegram channels and governance forums. It is important to remember that DAOs are ultimately collections of people. Even those DAOs that strive to automate governance as much as possible require some human intervention. Most DAOs have a mission or goal they are aiming to achieve. Gitcoin DAO's mission is to fund public goods, Lido DAO's is to offer decentralised staking, Forefront DAO's is to manage its media offerings and Friends With Benefits is a creative knowledge-sharing community. The DAO's mission and its governance structure will appear as documentation on its website or its governance forums, with a name like Constitution, Governance, or Manifesto, among others. *Third*, there is a financial component, most commonly in the form of a treasury that the community manages collectively. Funds can be kept in multi-signature wallets composed of highly trusted members who release funds or are automated fully with smart contracts. The treasury might be used to fund team budgets or perhaps to fund a community grant to a project or for marketing purposes or, well, whatever the DAO wants to do.

Roughly speaking, DAOs should be politically decentralised (D), meaning decision-making authority is spread among all participating members, rather than concentrated. DAOs are meant to express the broad consensus of its members, usually meaning the token holders of

DOI: 10.4324/9781003319603-5

the DAO. Autonomous (A) originally referred to the idea that DAO laws and rules would be encoded into smart contracts deployed on the blockchain and thereby immutable, meaning they could not be changed. However, this proved too restrictive in practice and nowadays it is more and more associated with the sense of autonomy the DAO structure grants to users,. Finally, the word organisation (O) is just a very generalised term meant to capture that a DAO can be for any purpose. Now, without wishing to scare you, the truth is nobody seems to quite know what DAOs are or how they should be implemented. There are endless debates between DAO theorists, practitioners and critics about "what a DAO is" and what constitutes real decentralisation. My approach is therefore to give you enough historical context and framing that you could participate in those debates and participate in a real DAO in the future.

Early History of Decentralised Autonomous Organisations (DAOs)

The idea of a DAO precedes its modern implementation by a number of years. The earliest conceptualisation is the Decentralised Autonomous Corporation (DAC), as proposed by Dan Larimer in 2013. Larimer theorised a blockchain like Bitcoin or Ethereum that is governed like a company or corporation. Larimer suggested:

> Think of a crypto-currency as shares in a Decentralized Autonomous Corporation (DAC) where the source code defines the bylaws. The goal of the DAC is to earn a profit for the shareholders by performing valuable services for the free market. With this goal in mind set out to maximize shareholder value at every stage as you design the bylaws that govern operation of the DAC.[1]

In the Ethereum white paper, Buterin expanded the definition of the DAC to the more generalised and now commonly accepted term Decentralised Autonomous Organisation (DAO). DAOs are introduced as a possible application that could be built on Ethereum and are defined as follows:

> The general concept of a "decentralized organization" is that of a virtual entity that has a certain set of members or shareholders which, perhaps with a 67% majority, have the right to spend the entity's funds and modify its code.[2]

In Buterin's model, DAOs are seen as one of the possible use cases for Ethereum. DAO members can create smart contracts on the Ethereum blockchain that enable community governance. In essence, a community with a specific goal can use smart contracts to manage funds and codify organisational rules together.

The DAO Hack

It might seem unusual to devote a section to a particular project, but The DAO is arguably the most controversial moment in Ethereum history. It is crucial to understand that The DAO represents the original sense of what people wanted DAOs to become, but also that this sense is now superseded and is no longer popular, although some argue a true DAO should follow its purely on-chain model. The DAO was originally proposed in early 2016 and was described variously as a decentralised fundraising mechanism or a decentralised venture capital fund.[3] The DAO smart contract encoded a business logic where users could purchase DAO tokens with ETH and then use these DAO tokens to vote on what The DAO should invest in. Here is how DuPont puts it in a famous ethnographic account of The DAO:

> ... DAO voting members would have significant control over projects. Since proposals were expected to be as transparent as possible (ideally, with their operational logic programmed into the blockchain), DAO voting members would directly control an organization by voting for (i.e., funding) specific decisions.[4]

A panel of "curators," featuring high-profile Ethereum members, was also set up to ensure projects were above board. All in all, the project appeared to have much going for it: a novel concept in line with blockchain principles, a clear business case and community support, including Ethereum co-founders and influential figures.

The DAO crowd sale launched in April 2016 and ended in May 2016. The DAO raised approximately 12 million ETH or $250 million at the time. This is the equivalent of 14% of all ETH in circulation at the time. However, on June 17, 2016, The DAO was the subject of a hack. The hack exploited a feature that allowed users to opt out of investments they didn't like. To opt out, users called a split function or a command to separate out their funds from the main DAO funds. Unfortunately, the logic of the split function could be exploited to keep calling it recursively, allowing the hacker to keep withdrawing over and over. The hacker managed to exploit The DAO to the tune of 3.6 million ETH or $55 million.

The DAO hack presented the nascent Ethereum community with a dilemma. Up to 20,000 people had invested in The DAO and the story had drawn considerable media attention because it was the largest crowd sale in history at the time. The damage was extensive enough that it raised the spectre of the ultimate taboo subject in blockchain cultures, to change the blockchain history. Blockchains are supposed to be *tamper-resistant* or *immutable*, meaning the history of the blockchain cannot be reverted. However, there is an important caveat here. When we call blockchains immutable we usually mean no central authority can overpower the rest of the stakeholders in a blockchain community and, for example, reverse a transaction. We are thinking of a hostile adversary who is trying to manipulate the blockchain for selfish purposes. Yet, it is always possible for blockchain stakeholders to violate immutability if the majority agrees it is in the best interest of the blockchain's health. It cannot be stressed enough how this is the nuclear option, the absolute last resort. The crisis involved must be seen as existential, as threatening the very existence of the project, which The DAO hack's prominence and amount of ETH involved did. After extensive discussion among the Ethereum stakeholders, the decision was reached to hard fork and reverse the effects of the hack. On July 20, 2016 (block 192,000), the Ethereum blockchain was hard forked. The hard fork did not roll back the chain to the time before the hack, but instead involved an "irregular state change" that transferred the stolen funds back to the DAO investors.[5] Users who wished to follow the new hard-forked version of the Ethereum blockchain had to upgrade their Ethereum nodes to software that recognises the irregular state change. Alternatively, users who disagreed could continue to follow the original, non-hard-forked version of the Ethereum blockchain. A small percentage of the community did precisely this and called this version Ethereum Classic. Ethereum, as we know it today, is the hard-forked version that includes the irregular state change.

The Modern DAO

The DAO concept was hit hard by The DAO hack and its consequences. However, the idea was kept alive by the trojan work of a small set of DAO enthusiasts. Notable examples are MakerDAO and MetaCartel, who pioneered many of the methods we'll encounter later, such as delegation and quorums. This eventually led to a renaissance of the DAO concept that reached fruition in 2021.

Modern DAOs can be made for any purpose, but over time certain types of DAOs have come to dominate the landscape. These are:

Infrastructural DAOs: These DAOs are dedicated to maintaining an important infrastructure within the wider Ethereum ecosystem, often with a focus on open source. Examples include ENS DAO, a DAO dedicated to the Ethereum Name Service domain name system of the Ethereum blockchain and Gitcoin DAO, which funds public goods in the Ethereum ecosystem.

Financial DAOs: These are found in a niche area of the Ethereum ecosystem known as Decentralised Finance (DeFi). DeFi DAOs govern decentralised finance products and services.

Creative DAOs: These DAOs are run by Non-Fungible Token (NFT) creators, curators, and collectors. They are built around blockchain art subcultures, such as NFT projects like the Meebits DAO or collecting the work of a particular artist, like PleasrDAO. Other examples include DAOs focused on connecting creatives working in the blockchain space, such as Friends with Benefits.

Let's examine the central elements of the modern DAO. I have modelled this outline on what I consider a highly representative DAO, Gitcoin DAO. In particular, I have focused on Gitcoin DAO as it ran between May 2021 and April 2022, which was the golden age of DAO development and innovation. Since there are over 10,000 DAOs in existence at the time of writing this template, I cannot hope to capture them all. Each DAO should be treated as unique, but they will *roughly* correspond to my Gitcoin DAO-inspired template. In this template, we tend to find technical, social and financial components.

Technical Components

The cornerstone of DAO technology is the governance token. *Governance tokens* confer membership and voting rights to DAO participants. They are usually ERC-20 fungible tokens, but can also be ERC-721 non-fungible tokens (see Chapter 7). DAO voting is often 1 token equals 1 vote. This means a user with 1 million tokens has a much larger voting power proportionally to a user with 100 votes. Governance tokens are often airdropped. An airdrop, in this context, is when early adopters of a protocol are rewarded with tokens. Once an airdrop is complete, the governance token can be purchased on the open market.

The next set of technologies are those that facilitate the governance or voting process. The stage after the discussion is a formal Snapshot vote. Snapshot enables DAOs to create a "space" associated with the DAO's Ethereum Name System (ENS) address.[6] The DAO then customises the space to fit their desired voting criteria. For example, a space's voting criteria might state a user needs 50,000 tokens to be eligible to create a proposal. Snapshot queries the blockchain at a certain block to create its snapshot of token holders. Second, when a voter interacts with the Snapshot UI, it will gather relevant information – their token holdings, how they voted – and then send a signature request asking them to confirm that the information is correct. A signature request, in this context, is a message an Ethereum EOA can sign in agreement. Signing a request does not require gas and this is why Snapshot is an off-chain or gasless voting system. When the user signs the message, Snapshot will then process this information using traditional

Web 2.0 database management tools (APIs, Node.js, MySQL). These activities are also recorded on a decentralised Peer-to-Peer (P2P) file-sharing service known as the InterPlanetary File System (IPFS).[7] The snapshot and the signature request are the only parts of Snapshot that use the Ethereum blockchain. This eliminates the need for users to make transactions requiring gas or the need to store data on the blockchain. Many DAOs use Snapshot as their only voting tool and then a set of trusted members will implement the results, such as releasing funds from a multisig-controlled treasury wallet. Others use Snapshot votes as a temperature check to gauge overall sentiment, before moving to fully on-chain votes.

Many DAOs prefer to have fully "on-chain" voting meaning they use smart contracts directly for governance. The most popular governance smart contracts, pioneered by DeFi protocols Compound and Uniswap, are Governor Alpha and Timelock (usually used together). DAOs will fork these template contracts and customise them according to their own needs. Governor Alpha is a smart contract that facilitates on-chain voting. The Governor contract will stipulate a threshold of token holdings for eligibility to create a proposal. It will also stipulate a threshold for voting eligibility. The proposal will adhere to the contract's defined voting period and quorum. Importantly, Governor votes concern executable code, most commonly a transfer of funds (e.g. to fund a DAO team, known as workstreams). The treasury funds are held in the associated Timelock smart contract. When a Governor vote succeeds, the code execution is queued up in Timelock and after a short queue delay period, an EOA can trigger the executable code, such as transferring funds to an address. Since direct on-chain voting can be somewhat intimidating, many DAOs use DAO management platforms such as Tally, which provides DAOs with a user-friendly frontend that backgrounds the governance smart contracts themselves.

Let's illustrate with the example of Gitcoin DAO. Gitcoin DAO is a popular DAO dedicated to funding open-source projects in the Ethereum ecosystem. Its main product is a set of smart contracts that allow Ethereans to donate to open-source public goods in the Ethereum ecosystem and then distribute those donations. Gitcoin DAO's governance suite includes a token (GTC) that confers voting rights and uses Snapshot votes to gauge community sentiment. Votes that don't involve treasury funds require only a Snapshot vote, but those that do involve funds require a fully on-chain vote using custom versions of Governor and Timelock.

Social Components

DAOs normally have a document (with a name like Constitution or Mission Statement) that outlines the DAO's governance process.

Of particular importance in these documents are the outlining of membership roles and governance processes.

Within a DAO there can be many different types of membership roles. The most basic role is the community member. Community members are simply users interested and actively participating in a DAO. You will often hear DAO discussions mention the community and this refers broadly to everyone interested in the DAO's mission. A *token holder* is a DAO member who has the right to participate in governance due to ownership of the DAO's governance token. In practice, most token holders do not participate in governance votes. This might be from a lack of interest, but even interested members might not have the time to fully review and assess governance proposals. This has led to the creation of the DAO delegate.

Delegates are DAO members who vote on behalf of DAO token holders. Through DAO tooling, a token holder can assign their tokens to a delegate, who will then represent them in the DAO, much like electing a politician. Delegates are often trusted users within the DAO or, more and more, are semi-/professional delegates. Delegates are expected to keep up with the latest events in the DAO, to have a deep understanding of how the DAO is structured, and to pay close and careful attention to proposals and votes. Delegates are chosen based on their perceived competency and value alignment. At any time, token holders can revoke their tokens from a delegate. Sometimes delegates are known as stewards.

In Gitcoin DAO, for example, token holders delegate to Stewards. Steward performance is tracked by a Health Card, a set of metrics that captures their activity across the DAO. All stewards are expected to attend a monthly review and high-performing Stewards can also be elected to the Steward Council, which meets bi-annually to perform an in-depth review. Another type of user is the contributor.

Contributors are highly engaged members that belong to one or more workstreams. They are akin to (but not the same as) employees in a traditional business organisation, but operating in a uniquely decentralised environment where the expectations of their role can be somewhat ambiguous. Some contributors may work full-time at the DAO or work part-time at multiple DAOs. Contributors work in what can variously be called workstreams, guilds, pods or sub-DAOs (among others). I'll stick with workstream here. A *workstream* is a sub-unit within a DAO dedicated to a specific set of tasks, such as marketing, governance, community, etc. Workstreams must first propose themselves to the community with a clear focus and a budget. For example, the marketing workstream might be required to report on their activities and request a new budget each season. Most DAOs operate in pre-defined time periods known as seasons.

Next are the governance processes. These are extremely important because they outline how votes are constructed, debated, ratified and then implemented. The governance process starts with a proposal from a community member. Proposals can be varied in content. There is no formal restriction on what a proposal should focus on, but the most common concern is new policies or procedures or changes to old ones; new product features or tools or tweaks to the current ones; and requests for funding (e.g. from workstreams). A proposal is posted to the discussion forum and formatted using the Improvement Proposal model pioneered in Bitcoin (Bitcoin Improvement Proposals or BIPs) and Ethereum governance (Ethereum Improvement Proposals or EIPs). Improvement Proposals are standardised or formalised documents for suggesting changes in a blockchain community.

For example, in Gitcoin DAO, members must post their proposals using the Gitcoin Community Proposal (GCP) format. The proposer provides a summary, an abstract, proposal motivation, the specification, benefits and drawbacks and then an explanation of what a yes or a no vote entails. Proposals must be discussed for at least five days and require input from a minimum of 5 Stewards unrelated to the proposal. Each DAO will have variations on what the Improvement Proposal is called, how they should be formatted, how long they must be discussed and whether delegates need to chime into the discussion. In smaller DAOs, in particular, the format is likely to be looser. An Improvement Proposal that has social support can then proceed to Snapshot or Governor (or both) in order to be accepted or rejected by the token holders/delegates.

As a final note here, it is worth noting most DAOs operate with a quite blunt one-token, one-vote model. This means large token holders are often in a position to dominate votes. This can often be the case when founders or early adopters control a large number of tokens and maintain control of the DAO even after transitioning to a DAO, known as progressive decentralisation. Despite this, the best-run DAOs manage to mitigate the worst effects of this model through delegation, which allows the community to select representatives to vote in ways that better align with their views. The adventurous may also find newer DAOs engaged in experimental governance mechanisms such as Quadratic Voting or Reputation-based voting.

Financial Components

DAOs operate a community treasury. The treasury funds come from different sources. In some cases, tokens from the original distribution are allocated to the DAO. In others, the DAO might have a revenue stream. Since a DAO's funds are often in their native token, a DAO can be impacted heavily, in both directions, by the value of its token. To mitigate this, many modern DAOs diversify their holdings. Governance votes are often related to financial matters, such as providing a budget for a workstream for a new season, hosting a conference or marketing. It is increasingly common for DAOs to offer grants that align with the project's aims or help build out the ecosystem. DAO treasuries can be managed using DAO tooling such as (Gnosis) Safe which allows a set of trusted members to form a multi-signature wallet that requires a quorum to release funds. Some treasuries are built directly into governance smart contracts and will automatically release funds contingent on voting results. Perhaps the most intriguing aspect of DAOs is that their treasuries are completely transparent. DAO treasury addresses are posted publicly and members can observe the funds using an Ethereum blockchain explorer.

The DAO model has been effectively used to raise funds on an *ad hoc* basis. In 2021, ConstitutionDAO was established as a single-purpose DAO to raise funds and bid on an original copy of the United States Constitution. While the bid failed, the DAO raised $47 million by selling its governance token, with members then voting on how best to proceed in the bid. Ukraine DAO and AssangeDAO were two other highly successful single-purpose DAOs that raised significant funds for activist purposes.

Since there is often a financial aspect to DAOs, they are sometimes attacked for their treasuries, from inside and out. The simplest is perhaps the rug pull. Rug pulls are when a DAO project raises or attracts funds and then abandons it, stealing the DAO's treasury. Another vector of attack is governance attacks. Governance attacks are when the DAO's own structure is used to manipulate the DAO for financial gain. In 2022, an attacker used a sophisticated transaction called a flash loan to access enough funds to make them the majority governance token stakeholder of the Beanstalk DAO. They then used their governance tokens to push through an on-chain vote that transferred a substantial sum from the Beanstalk treasury to themselves. In 2023, the Tornado Cash DAO suffered a similar fate when an attacker subtly inserted malicious code into a proposal that allowed them to take control of the DAO's treasury. Also in 2023, the Aragon Association was the victim of an attempted "treasury raid" where malicious actors attempted to co-opt its governance processes to steal funds.

Many DAOs manage a blockchain-based product or service in a similar way to a traditional centralised company. For example, the Aave DAO is responsible for managing a set of financial products and offerings that produce revenue for the DAO, including borrowing and lending (the Aave protocol), a stablecoin (GHO) and Aave Arc (institutional DeFi).

Apecoin DAO governs the ApeCoin cryptocurrency ecosystem. ApeCoin DAO is therefore concerned with furthering the success of ApeCoin by promoting the brand and providing grants that build a healthier ecosystem. LinksDAO offers its members exclusive benefits related to golfing, such as discounts at partner golf courses. Finally, it is worth stressing not all DAOs are money-oriented and many are simply communities built around mutual interests and knowledge-sharing.[8] For example, Boys Club World is a social DAO that uses off-chain voting to organise real-world events.

Notes

1 Larimer D (2013) Overpaying For Security. Available at: https://letstalkbitcoin.com/blog/post/is-bitcoin-overpaying-for-false-security
2 Buterin V (2014) Ethereum: A Next-Generation Smart Contract and Decentralized Application Platform. Available at: https://ethereum.org/669c9e2e2027310b6b 3cdce6e1c52962/Ethereum_Whitepaper_-_Buterin_2014.pdf.
3 For an excellent first-person history of The DAO see Laura Shin's podcast episode featuring three founding members: https://web.archive.org/web/20220301140058/https://www.youtube.com/watch?v=j0QnWhUUD1c Note that in this podcast the members stress they didn't see The DAO as an investment fund, but rather this framing was placed on it externally. However, for pedagogical reasons, I think a decentralised investment fund is nicely intuitive and worth sticking with.
4 DuPont Q (2017) Experiments in algorithmic governance: A history and ethnography of "The DAO," a failed decentralized autonomous organization. In: Campbell-Verduyn M (ed.) *Bitcoin and Beyond: Cryptocurrencies, Blockchains, and Global Governance.* London: Routledge, pp. 157–177. DOI: 10.4324/9781315211909-8, p. 160.
5 See *Ethereum Foundation Blog* (2016) Hard Fork Completed. Available at: https://blog.ethereum.org/2016/07/20/hard-fork-completed
6 An ENS is a readable domain name linked to an Ethereum address. For instance, Vitalik Buterin owns the EOA address 0xd8dA6BF26964aF9D 7eEd9e03E53415D37aA96045. The ENS domain name registered to this address is vitalik.eth, which is much easier to type. Anyone can link their EOA address to an ENS domain name if it is available, similar to registering a domain name on the traditional Internet.
7 The ENS domain contains a text record that points to a JSON file stored on the InterPlanetary File Sharing (IPFS) P2P network.
8 Recently, DAO theorist Stefen Deleveaux has proposed the concept of proto-DAOs, that better captures contemporary online communities that are in the process of becoming "full" DAOs, usually characterised by a looser, even fun attitude to DAO-building.

References

Buterin V (2014) Ethereum: A Next-Generation Smart Contract and Decentralized Application Platform. Available at: https://ethereum.org/669c9e2e2027310b 6b3cdce6e1c52962/Ethereum_Whitepaper_-_Buterin_2014.pdf.

DuPont Q (2017) Experiments in algorithmic governance: A history and ethnography of "The DAO," a failed decentralized autonomous organization. In: Campbell-Verduyn M (ed.) *Bitcoin and Beyond: Cryptocurrencies, Blockchains, and Global Governance*. London: Routledge, pp. 157–177. DOI: 10.4324/9781315211909-8, p. 160.

Ethereum Foundation Blog (2016) Hard Fork Completed. Available at: https://blog.ethereum.org/2016/07/20/hard-fork-completed

Larimer D (2013) Overpaying For Security. Available at: https://letstalkbitcoin.com/blog/post/is-bitcoin-overpaying-for-false-security

6   Decentralised Finance (DeFi)

Decentralised Finance (DeFi) is an ecosystem of protocols that enable permissionless and transparent finance. DeFi is designed to disintermediate traditional finance, but also centralised exchanges for Crypto assets. It achieves this by creating decentralised analogues to financial products and services created by traditional banks, payment processors, trading platforms and centralised exchanges. The most common products and services found in DeFi are stablecoins, Decentralised Exchanges (DEXs), Automated Market Makers (AMMs), Liquidity Pools (LPs), borrowing/lending protocols, oracles and bridges. The DeFi ecosystem is composed of a large number of smart contract protocols defining an underlying financial logic, e.g. to swap tokens, provide liquidity or bridge assets across blockchains. Most DeFi protocols have a user-friendly frontend for users to interact with via wallet software such as MetaMask, making them Decentralised Applications (dApps). The financial assets in the DeFi context are usually ETH, Ethereum's currency, and a vast number of ERC-20 fungible tokens built on Ethereum. *ERC-20* is the token standard for creating currencies or tokens on the Ethereum blockchain. Since the assets follow the same ERC-20 standard, DeFi protocols are highly interoperable with one another, called composability or "money lego." The experience for the end user is a certain freedom or frictionlessness as they move assets between different protocols without needing to interact with a centralised financial intermediary.

The DeFi community is somewhat contradictory in tone. Let's start with the positive. DeFi is defined against traditional financial institutions (TradFi). It sees TradFi as opaque, exclusionary and unfair. TradFi's problems are said to stem from centralisation or the consolidation of power and decision-making. TradFi is portrayed as full of gatekeepers who make it hard or even impossible to participate in banking and finance, whether this means complete exclusion ("the unbanked") or power asymmetries (such as insider knowledge). The idea is the little guy

DOI: 10.4324/9781003319603-6

stands no chance against the banks and Wall Street. In contrast, DeFi is presented as *permissionless* and *transparent* finance. You do not need permission to use a DeFi protocol. There are no Know Your Customer/ Anti-Money Laundering (KYC/AML) documents to upload and prove your identity. The unbanked can be involved. Power asymmetries are said to be undermined by how DeFi protocols operate transparently, since the smart contract logic exists on-chain, available for all to inspect. To its defenders, DeFi is an experiment in the democratisation of finance. Now the negative. DeFi culture is known for its degens (degenerates) who will recklessly "ape in" into any popular new DeFi protocol. Often it is exactly the little guy, the retail investor, who will get "rekt" here, perpetuating a cycle of financial ruthlessness. Further, it might be argued that the complexity of DeFi protocols renders them opaque too, but in the sense that the requisite technical knowledge and information is beyond the ken of most retail users. And we'll see all kinds of scams and hustles are rife in DeFi. As befitting a nascent finance ecosystem, there are trade-offs and you'll have to decide for yourself whether the message matches the reality.

DeFi Summer 2020

According to DeFi historian Brady Dale, the concept of DeFi coalesced around a 2018 "Decentralized Finance Meetup" that included "the Maker Foundation, Compound Labs, 0x, dYdX, Wyre."[1] A number of projects in the Ethereum ecosystem recognised at this event that they were all working on similar financial smart contract protocols or dApps. However, it was not until DeFi Summer 2020 that a coherent field called Decentralised Finance (DeFi) truly emerged.[2] This era was characterised by a remarkable flurry of creation that generated the primitives underpinning DeFi today. Let's run through these now.

Stablecoins

A *stablecoin* is a cryptocurrency or token that is pegged one-to-one with a fiat currency, such as the US dollar or Euro. 50 USDC, a popular stablecoin, is worth $50. 150 DAI, another popular stablecoin, is worth $150. Or they *should* be, we'll touch on this more later. Stablecoins have two main benefits. First, they help offset the infamous volatility of Crypto assets. If the markets are too unpredictable a user might decide to swap their Crypto assets for stablecoin "dollars." By "dollar" we mean a unit, typically an ERC-20 fungible token, representing a dollar. Stablecoins also allow users to move these stablecoin dollars between exchanges, e.g. to take advantage of arbitrage opportunities, which are price differences across exchanges. Second, stablecoins allow people to be paid in "dollars" or "euros." Imagine you hire someone to work on a project in March and the price of 1 ETH is $2,000. But then the market improved in April and now 1 ETH is worth $3,000. This is not ideal! Instead, you could agree to pay $2,000 USDC or DAI, which will remain stable. You can likely see how useful it is to have a representation of fiat (or government-backed) currencies on the blockchain. Traditionally, the major stablecoins have been centralised ones associated with exchanges or consortia, such as Tether's USDT or Centre's USDC. Similar to banks, these exchanges and consortia guarantee or back the stablecoins with reserves. This means I can always, in theory, redeem 1 USDT for $1 or 1 USDC for $1. I say in theory because you have to trust these centralised stablecoin backers do in fact have those reserves, which in this industry they might not! Stablecoins are not niche or obscure, but make up a large percentage of the overall Crypto assets market capitalisation.

In 2014, Rune Christensen started working on the concept of a *decentralised stablecoin* and established a DAO in 2015 to bring it into reality, called MakerDAO.[3] The stablecoin, known as DAI, did not appear until 2017. Decentralised stablecoins are managed by a combination of smart contract logic and an associated company and/or DAO. Typically, the smart contract logic includes a process for minting stablecoins in exchange for locking collateral, normally overcollateralized. In effect, you provide more collateral than what you are borrowing. For example, to borrow $50 DAI, you might need to lock up $150 worth of ETH. Borrowers must also pay an interest fee while borrowing. Most decentralised stablecoin protocols will include a mechanism to liquidate your position if your collateral drops in value and you don't add more collateral to compensate. The smart contract/s underpinning a DeFi protocol are managed by a company and/or a Decentralised Autonomous Organisation (DAO). For instance, MakerDAO is composed of members holding the Maker (MKR) governance token. MKR confers voting rights on the holder. The MakerDAO community votes about how much collateral is required to borrow, what collateral is accepted, what the interest rate should be, etc. Aave DAO members manage their GHO stablecoin in a similar manner. Usually, the interest fees go to the DAO's treasury, which can then be used to fund new projects, pay workstream salaries, host events or create grants.

Another decentralised stablecoin approach is the algorithmic stablecoins. Algorithmic stablecoins are smart contract protocols that maintain a fiat peg through dynamic rebalancing mechanisms. Algorithmic stablecoins are designed to dynamically rebalance with a mint-and-burn mechanism built on a relationship between a stablecoin and an associated token. For instance, TerraUSD (UST) was a stablecoin associated with the Terra (LUNA) token. Holders could redeem 1 UST for $1 in the market value of LUNA and vice versa. Whenever the price of UST deviated from $1, say to $1.01, holders of LUNA could burn LUNA in exchange for UST. Note there is a tiny arbitrage opportunity here of $0.01 that might add up at scale, representing the incentive to burn LUNA. Since a rise above $1 indicates demand, the idea is that minting more UST will increase supply, bringing the price back down to $1. Conversely, when UST deviated below $1, say to $0.99, holders of UST could burn UST for a $1 equivalent of the market value of LUNA. In this case, they are getting a tiny bit more LUNA than they could on the open market. This would decrease the supply of UST and restore the peg. In each case, the minter or burner benefits from the small arbitrage difference in price.

On occasion, stablecoins can de-peg or lose their peg to the fiat asset. De-pegging can be caused by market volatility, regulatory pressure, concern about reserves, smart contract bugs or bad design. Once a peg is broken, the loss of faith in a stablecoin can result in mass sell-offs of the stablecoin or swapping into alternative stablecoins, further breaking the peg. In 2022, TerraUSD (UST) collapsed in a "death spiral" when users lost faith in its rebalancing mechanism, leading to a mass contagion event that collapsed the overall Crypto asset markets. The collapse of Terra has discredited the idea of algorithmic stablecoins. In 2023, Circle's USDC survived a serious de-pegging event when a major holder of USDC reserves (8% of all reserves), Silicon Valley Bank, collapsed. Despite falling as low as $0.87, USDC nonetheless returned to its $1 peg after a week, showing that overall confidence in USDC remained.

Decentralised Exchanges (DEXs)

Let's start negatively, by making clear what DEXs are not, namely centralised exchanges. Centralised exchanges are trading platforms for Crypto assets run by companies. This definition is a bit clunky, but it's important in this chapter to stress these are run as traditional companies, like Revolut, Visa or Robinhood, but for Crypto assets. Centralised exchanges allow users to buy Crypto assets directly from the exchange with the option of using fiat currencies (bank transfers, credit/debit cards, etc.). The exchange sources the liquidity for these purchases through reserves, but also uses market makers, who provide liquidity to exchanges wholesale. Centralised exchanges also allow users to trade with each other using an order book model. In fact, it is not uncommon to hear centralised exchanges defined as order book exchanges. An order book sees users that wish to sell matched with users that wish to buy, and vice versa. Significantly, the order book software underpinning the trading platform is not a smart contract, but custom software directly under the control of the exchange. Users do not have transparent insight into how exchanges operate and essentially must trust the reputation of the company. Further, once users deposit funds onto exchanges they no longer have custody over those assets, the exchange does. Centralised exchanges are regulated – though sometimes play fast and loose with regulators – and therefore require customers to provide documentation, to fulfil KYC/AML laws. This is especially true when users deposit real dollars or euros via bank transfer or debit/credit card. The most well-known centralised exchanges are Coinbase and Binance. You might remember the infamous collapse of the centralised exchange FTX and its CEO Sam Bankman-Fried, who partly made his name by betting big on early DeFi protocols. Many retail investors like to use centralised exchanges because they don't want to control their own private keys, effectively outsourcing wallet security. Most blockchain veterans encourage users to not hold assets on centralised exchanges due to their history of hacks and collapses. The Bitcoiners like to say "not your keys, not your coins" and when they're right, they're right.

Decentralised Exchange (DEX) is an umbrella term for DeFi smart contract protocols that allow users to swap Crypto assets. In Ethereum's case, this means ERC-20 tokens. DEXs are permissionless and require only an EOA account to connect to the smart contract, usually via a front end. The underlying financial logic of the DEX protocol is transparent since it is an on-chain smart contract. The code is there on Etherscan for any user to inspect, if they are capable. The truth, of course, is most of us aren't capable of understanding the code and here again we must trust those who do. Finally, DEXs are non-custodial because they do not hold assets on your behalf like a centralised exchange. The relationship is between the end-user and the smart contract. This does not mean your assets are safe, but just that they are safe from centralised exchange collapse. While many DEXs started as companies, most, especially the more popular ones – Uniswap, SushiSwap, dYdX, 1Inch – now operate on a hybrid company/DAO model or are completely DAO-run.

Let's look at some of the DEX models you are likely to come across in DeFi.

Initial Coin Offering (ICO)

Let's start with a dishonourable mention, the cursed ICO era of Ethereum history. An *Initial Coin Offering (ICO)* is a fundraising mechanism where users send ETH to a contract in exchange for a project's newly created token. This is really all there is to the idea and, in theory, it is actually a pretty efficient way to launch a project.

Unfortunately, the simple elegance of the model opens it to rug pulls. In an *ICO rug pull*, extremely common in the 2017 era, the project would simply take the ETH, leaving investors holding a worthless token for a project that will never be created. This discredited the ICO model. However, it is worth mentioning that the ICO model did enable some legitimate projects. For example, Aave, a major DEX, was originally funded by an ICO in 2017. Other honourable mentions go to Filecoin (file sharing), Chainlink (oracle service) and Rocket Pool (decentralised staking). The Ethereum pre-sale could be seen as a quasi-ICO, in that to buy ETH originally users had to send BTC to an address and then later receive ETH. However, I think the term pre-sale works well enough, without muddying the waters with a contentious term like ICO.

Automated Market Makers (AMMs)

Among the most well-known Decentralised Exchanges (DEXs) are *Automated Market Makers (AMMs)*.[4] On Ethereum, AMMs are smart contract protocols for swapping ERC-20 assets. When using an AMM, a user will normally interact with a user-friendly frontend for a set of smart contracts. A smart contract protocol with a frontend like this is known as a Decentralised Application (dApp). Connecting your wallet software, such as the MetaMask browser wallet, you input the swap you wish to make, e.g. I want to swap 0.5 ETH for the equivalent in USDC. To make this trade I will pay the AMM a transaction fee. Uniswap, to pick the most popular AMM, charges 0.3% per swap. It is important to wrap your head around how different this model is from a centralised exchange. When you use a DEX you are interacting with a smart contract on the Ethereum blockchain. The relation is between you and this smart contract. The website frontend mediates but fundamentally you are calling functions, like swapExactETHForTokens, from the DEX smart contract. Then that transaction is sent to the Ethereum validators for inclusion in a block. There's no centralised exchange intermediary involved. The question you might have is, in the absence of other traders, exchange reserves or market makers, where is the liquidity for your swap coming from? The answer is Liquidity Pools (LPs).

Liquidity Pools (LPs)

Liquidity Pools (LPs) are smart contracts holding Crypto assets for use in Decentralised Exchanges (DEXs). A liquidity pool might be managed by the same protocol that uses it (e.g. Uniswap, SushiSwap) or it might be run by specialist liquidity pool providers (e.g. Bancor, Curve). Liquidity Providers (also called LPs!) are users who supply assets to the pool and in return receive a token, called an LP token. LP tokens represent my deposited assets, but also any rewards I accrue for participating in the pool. The rewards primarily come from the AMM transaction fees and are distributed proportionally to liquidity providers. If there is $20,000 of assets in the pool and I provide $2,000 then my share is 10% and I'll receive 10% of the transaction fees. When I withdraw I get back my deposited assets plus the fees I earned. The act of providing assets to liquidity pools in exchange for transaction fees is known as *liquidity mining*.

During DeFi summer, AMMs/liquidity pools often incentivised users to abandon their current pools and switch to a new one by offering a token on top of the transaction fees. There is even an attack, the vampire attack, where a new DEX simply copies another, but with added incentives, famously performed by SushiSwap on Uniswap in 2020. The tactics are less aggressive today, but it is not uncommon to receive an airdropped token for providing liquidity to a new AMM/ liquidity pool. When a user moves between different liquidity pools to chase the best yield this is known as *yield farming*. There also exist protocols that "professionalise" yield farming, such as Yearn. Users deposit assets into these yield farming protocols, which then put their assets to work according to strategies, e.g. switching assets from different liquidity pools depending on which offers the current best rate. An added bonus of liquidity pools is that new projects can bootstrap themselves by creating a liquid market for their token through liquidity pools. They do not need to be traded on centralised exchanges, though successful ones will be.

How do AMMs and liquidity pools know how many tokens to send you and at what price? AMMs use custom algorithms in conjunction with liquidity pools to arrive at prices. The most well-known AMM algorithm is the Constant Product Market Maker (CPMM). It's the algorithm behind Uniswap and therefore likely the most used AMM algorithm of all time. The Constant Product Market Maker (CPMM) algorithm is $x * y = k$. The x and y refer to the assets in the liquidity pool and k what is known as the constant or invariant.

Let's imagine a *simplified* example of a liquidity pool that lets people swap ETH and USDC.

The creator of the ETH-USDC pool sets the price of the assets at the beginning. Let's imagine ETH is currently trading at $1000 on centralised exchanges like Binance or Coinbase. I am a trader who wants to swap 1 ETH for what I expect will be around $1000. The pool creator will initially put equal amounts of each asset into the pool: 200 ETH and 200,000 USDC. The constant or invariant of our ETH-USDC pool is the sum of these assets: $200 \times 200,000 = 40,000,000$. The secret to how AMMs work is that the reserves for each asset will be rebalanced after a swap to remain at k (40,000,000). If I want to make this swap I'll have to send 1 ETH into the pool. The pool now has 201 ETH. We need to rebalance the assets to maintain the product. This is accomplished by dividing 40,000,000 by the new balance of 201 ETH to arrive at 199,004.97 USDC (rounded down). Because that's the ratio that maintains the constant: $201 \times 199,004.97 = 40,000,000$. Now the algorithm subtracts the new USDC amount from the original USDC amount to arrive at how many USDC to send me. 200,000 USDC (original amount) – 199,004.97 (new balance) = 995.03 USDC. From this amount, AMMs can also arrive at a price. We divide the original amount by the new balance. In this case, 200,000% 198,000 tells us that USDC in this pool now trades at \$1.01. To find the new price of ETH in this pool we divide the original amount of 200 ETH by the new amount of 201 ETH to get 0.99 ETH. There's less USDC now in the pool so it trades a little higher; there's more ETH in the pool so it trades a little lower.

Arbitrageurs are traders who take advantage of price discrepancies across exchanges, whether centralised or decentralised. For example, imagine there is a price difference between ETH on an ETH-USDC pool on Uniswap and Binance, with ETH trading higher on Uniswap. Arbitrageurs will buy ETH on Uniswap and then sell it on Binance. The differences in prices from swaps, especially large ones that tilt the ratio, are known as *price impacts*. *Price slippage* refers to the difference between expected price and actual price. For example, if you are on Uniswap and thinking about a swap for a few minutes you might have the transaction ready to go, but not initiate it. Then when you do initiate it there might have been a swap from someone else that caused a price impact. The price has "slipped" from what you intended and what will actually happen. It also tends to occur in illiquid or imbalanced pools where any trade causes substantial price changes. Most DEXs will limit price slippage and warn users, but it is also possible to maximise slippage, in situations where it is either not important or expedient. A final concept, that is a little advanced, but worth knowing is impermanent loss. *Impermanent loss* is when a liquidity provider would have been better off holding an asset than supplying it to a pool.

Borrowing and Lending Platforms

The next popular Decentralised Exchanges (DEXs) are borrowing/lending platforms. Luckily, this is the easiest and most intuitive DeFi concept to understand. *Borrowing/lending platforms* are smart contract protocols that enable users to borrow and lend Crypto assets. Simplified somewhat, users deposit assets as collateral into a smart contract and then borrow assets against their collateral. The borrower's position will be overcollateralized, meaning you will need to deposit more assets than you borrow. For example, if I want to borrow 500 USDC then I may need to have the equivalent of 1500 USDC in ETH, for example, locked into the borrowing/lending protocol. Some platforms might have a timeframe to return assets, but most are open-ended. However, if the collateral deposited begins to depreciate – say you used ETH and the market crashes – then you might be liquidated and your assets auctioned. The borrowed assets are originally supplied by users to liquidity pools, who earn interest, represented in LP tokens. Many borrowing/lending protocols include some kind of "safety module" where users stake the protocol's governance stake in exchange for interest, but where those staked assets can be used in emergency events, such as the catastrophic collapse of an asset used for collateral in the protocol. A more technically advanced type of loan is also possible, called a flash loan. A *flash loan* is an un-collateralised loan that takes place within a single block, usually knitting together a series of complex smart contract interactions that take advantage of an arbitrage opportunity. The condition of a flash loan is the assets borrowed must be repaid at the end of the transaction within the same block.

Derivatives Exchanges

Derivatives Exchanges are smart contract protocols allowing users to trade complex financial instruments like perpetual futures, options, etc. These are relatively easy to understand since they mimic the more advanced financial instruments found on traditional trading platforms, but with smart contract logic. Some Derivatives Exchanges allow users to trade synthetic assets, which are tokenised representations of assets like commodities, stocks and bonds.

DeFi Infrastructure

Oracles

Blockchain oracles are third-party or middleware services that provide external or off-chain data to the blockchain. Blockchains like Ethereum don't have an internal mechanism for sourcing external data, e.g. price feeds. Instead, they use oracles. Blockchain oracles usually have two parts, on-chain smart contracts that accept requests for data and then off-chain networks that source and then authenticate data to return. Imagine I initiate a transaction on a borrowing/lending protocol to borrow 1 ETH. The borrowing/lending protocol will call an oracle smart contract requesting the current price of 1 ETH to facilitate my transaction. The oracle smart contract will then pull this data in from its external feeds and relay the information back, enabling me to borrow 1 ETH at current market rates. Now, you might spot how the external relation could be an issue here. What if the oracle smart contract is pulling current prices in from a centralised or third-party source? The reliance of oracles on centralised sources for data is known as the *oracle problem*. Contemporary oracle protocols, such as Chainlink (LINK), have overcome the problem by pulling the data from their own external decentralised network. With Chainlink, the oracle smart contract is not just pulling data in from centralised price feeds, but communicates with the Chainlink network of decentralised nodes, which are aggregated into a final result and posted back to the on-chain smart contract.

Bridges

Bridges enable cross-chain transfers between blockchains. Bridges can be trusted – meaning they are operated by trusted third parties – or trustless – meaning they are decentralised smart contract protocols. Bridges can be built between two Layer 1 blockchains like Bitcoin and Ethereum or Ethereum and Avalanche. Or they can be built between a Layer 1 blockchain and one of its Layer 2 blockchains. As we'll see in a future chapter, Ethereum has a number of Layer 2s that users can bridge to. Here we stick with the Layer 1 version of cross-chain bridging. Bridging usually involves a mechanism called lock-and-mint. Let's imagine we want to bridge some BTC to the Ethereum blockchain. The Bitcoin and Ethereum blockchain are not compatible. I can't just send BTC to an Ethereum address! In 2019, a consortium created Wrapped Bitcoin (WBTC) to solve this problem. Step one is to lock our BTC by sending it to a specific address controlled by one of the Wrapped Bitcoin partners. We pay a fee for the service, of course. The partner will then mint the equivalent amount of ETH on the Ethereum blockchain, using a smart contract. The newly minted version of your locked BTC will be an ERC-20 token called WBTC. Your BTC is "wrapped" with this token format on Ethereum. You can now use BTC on Ethereum! There is usually also a process where you can burn your bridged assets on the second chain, to unlock them on the first. This lock-and-mint mechanism is not limited to WBTC. There are bridges for moving ETH over to Avalanche, Cosmos, etc. And vice versa. More commonly on Ethereum users can bridge between Layer 1 and the many Layer 2s such as Optimism or Arbitrum.

DeFi DAO Governance

DeFi protocols can be either companies, company/DAO hybrids or DAOs. Among the most popular protocols – such as Uniswap and Aave – the hybrid model is preferred. The model of transitioning from a company or corporate structure into a Decentralised Autonomous Organisation (DAO), whether in part or completely, is called *progressive decentralisation*. The transition is usually implemented by distributing a token to the community – perhaps early adopters or through a pre-sale – which then functions as the DAO's governance token. For instance, the UNI token was airdropped in 2020 to early users of Uniswap Automated Market Maker (AMM) and liquidity pools. UNI holders thereby became the Uniswap DAO and vote on matters related to the protocol. But Uniswap Labs, the company behind the creation of Uniswap, did not simply disappear. The Labs and the DAO operate side-by-side, in a hybrid model, with Uniswap Labs continuing to produce new versions of the protocol. The model can vary from protocol to protocol. In Aave's case, progressive decentralisation occurred in 2020 as well, and the process is called Aavenomics. Holders of AAVE form the Aave DAO and manage the Aave protocol and the GHO stablecoin. However, the original Aave company and related companies still exist, but are now funded by the Aave DAO treasury as service providers. Many DAOs start out with looser, non-corporate structures, consisting of like-minded people who then launch a DAO, like Tree DAO. In one famous case, Yearn, the project was originally the work of a single individual, Andre Cronje, who then allowed the project to transition into a DAO model.

Total Value Locked (TVL)

When we discuss DeFi protocols, regardless of their organisational structure, there is a metric called Total Value Locked (TVL) that refers to the total amount of value associated with the protocol. The term is not a formal one, but used by DeFi industry websites (e.g. DeFiLlama) and should not be taken as strictly defined yet. However, TVL can and usually includes the market capitalisation of the protocol's associated governance token, the DAO's treasury, assets staked in the protocol, assets provided to liquidity pools, assets borrowed and any revenue generated. This can be quite individualised – a stablecoin protocol's TVL is measured differently from an AMM's – even though all the different types of protocols tend to get ranked alongside one another. Regardless, it is a useful metric for getting a snapshot of a protocol when originally researching it (as you should, intensively).

DeFi Risks and Opportunities

Since DEXs are smart contract protocols, they can contain *smart contract bugs* that hackers exploit. In 2021, the borrowing/lending protocol Compound accidentally emitted $90m worth of its COMP tokens to its users due to a smart contract bug. Also in 2021, an attacker exploited a pricing bug in the Cream Finance protocol to steal $130m of CREAM tokens. And there are countless examples we could draw on here. In a *rug pull*, the team outright steals the funds themselves. In these cases, the team might work hard at presenting a legitimate face, even operating as a DeFi protocol should, thereby gaining the confidence of users. They might then attract liquidity to their pool, for example, before people realise the smart contract contains code enabling the developers will pull the liquidity.

You may have noticed in this chapter I've tried to scare you a little bit about the dangers of Decentralised Finance (DeFi). That's good, because it's a ruthless place and you will need your wits about you. However, you might be wondering, if it's so risky why do people still use DeFi? It's because if you are a cautious – and I mean *cautious* – and conservative user of DeFi there are benefits and opportunities to be had. First, using an AMM DEX means you do not need to use centralised exchanges, reducing your exposure to exchange collapse and hacks. Second, becoming a Liquidity Provider is a useful way to put your assets to productive work, provided you understand they are at *risk* by the very fact that they are working in an experimental financial ecosystem! In other words, you should not use DeFi as your primary and certainly not your only way to make money. You should presume that at *any time* your funds may disappear. Third, an experienced user can take advantage of opportunities through borrowing and lending protocols, with the same presumption of high risk in mind. Much of this will come down to, ironically, how much trust you put in the people operating the protocol, one of the many paradoxes of the ecosystem.

Notes

1 See Dale B (2020) One Billion, Two Billion, Three Billion, Four? DeFi's Knocking on TradFi's Door. Available at: https://www.coindesk.com/tech/2020/07/28/one-billion-two-billion-three-billion-four-defis-knocking-on-tradfis-door/
2 I leave it up to future DeFi scholars to uncover a deeper history and suspect they will find many prototypes of DeFi before 2020. MakerDAO is an obvious example, with roots going back to 2014. There were also early examples of Decentralised Exchanges (DEXs) such as EtherDelta and OasisDEX. I take DeFi "proper" to refer to the suite of protocols that emerged in DeFi Summer 2020.
3 Around the same time, in 2014, Dan Larimer's project BitShares created BitUSD. Since BitUSD never quite caught on I've decided to focus on

MakerDAO, since it is arguably the best example of a successful and functional decentralised stablecoin.

4 You may also hear Constant Function Market Makers (CFMM), with constant function referring to the algorithms underpinning AMMs.

Reference

Dale B (2020) One Billion, Two Billion, Three Billion, Four? DeFi's Knocking on TradFi's Door. Available at: https://www.coindesk.com/tech/2020/07/28/one-billion-two-billion-three-billion-four-defis-knocking-on-tradfis-door/

7 Non-Fungible Tokens (NFTs)

Non-Fungible Tokens (NFTs) are digital tokens that represent unique assets on a blockchain. Within a blockchain context, an NFT is seen to confer ownership of an item to a specific Externally-Owned Account (EOA), an Ethereum user account. NFTs are created as either single items or individual items within a collection. The business logic governing the NFT collection is established within a smart contract. Developers launch the collection by deploying it to the Ethereum blockchain, where it becomes a contract account that any EOA can interact with. In practice, an NFT is usually a numbered token that has an associated link or pointer to some metadata, such as an image or a set of traits. This metadata is not commonly stored on the Ethereum blockchain, which can be expensive to use for storage. In theory, NFTs can be used to represent anything, but in practice, there is a cluster of popular use cases. These are as follows:

Collectibles, especially Profile Picture (PFP) collections.
One-off artworks by individual artists.
In-game items, especially in the metaverse.
Brand items, such as loyalty cards or fan access.

Culturally speaking, NFT collectors are often enthusiasts who enjoy collecting distinctive or rare items, akin to Pokémon card or movie memorabilia collectors. This is not to suggest that the NFT community are unaware of Ethereum's values or how its infrastructure works. In fact, NFT users are often among the most pragmatic Ethereans and are usually well acquainted with the intricacies of software wallets, such as handling their own private keys or minting NFTs directly from smart contracts. On the negative side, the NFT world is also blighted by cybercriminals targeting new retail investors, especially through social engineering tactics, and there is an endless output of low-quality NFT projects. Like an antique collector at a boot sale, the rookie NFT

DOI: 10.4324/9781003319603-7

collector will need to be vigilant to sort the wheat from the chaff. NFTs typically (but not always) involve two main components. First, there is a technical component in the form of the NFT smart contract, commonly based on a standard called ERC-721. Second, there is a financial component, especially the central role NFT marketplaces play, but also in relation to traditional business concerns such as branding and copyright.

Fungible versus Non-Fungible

Non-fungible means an item is not fungible. Fungible items are items that are exchangeable like-for-like. We typically consider currencies and commodities to be fungible. For example, any dollar is exchangeable for any other (presuming neither is damaged). If I deposited a $100 bill into a bank one day and then withdrew $100 a week later, it is not necessary to receive the exact note back. Dollar bills are fungible. The same is true for a commodity like oil. Any barrel, presuming no damage, is the same as any other. I'm not particularly interested in any *specific* barrel of oil. Closer to home, cryptocurrencies are also fungible. If I deposit 10 bitcoin to the Coinbase exchange one day and then withdraw them a week later, it does not matter that I get back the specific 10 bitcoin I deposited. They are completely fungible. The same holds for the ERC-20 tokens built on Ethereum. *ERC-20* is the token standard for creating currencies or tokens on the Ethereum block-chain. For example, we might want to create an ERC-20 token celebrating Almonds (ALM). Each ALM token will be equivalent in nature. It won't matter whether I send you this or that batch of ALM tokens. The same is true for the numerous ERC-20 tokens built on Ethereum, like Shiba Inu (SHIB) or USD Coin (USDC) or West Ham (HAM).

Non-fungible items are unique items. The specificity of a non-fungible item matters. This uniqueness can come in two senses. *First,* non-fungible uniqueness can mean there is just one of the item. The Mona Lisa is a non-fungible item that was created once and is not exchangeable like-for-like with anything else. The Mona Lisa is "one of a kind" and an attendee of EthCC Paris will probably take a detour to view it. The *second* sense of non-fungibility refers to uniqueness within a wider set. For example, if I want to attend a Justin Bieber concert, I need to buy a ticket, but not all tickets are the same. There might be 50,000 tickets sold, but some hold unique properties: one might be closer to the stage, another further from the stage, etc. They are all Justin Bieber tickets, but I don't consider them like-for-like. Another example would be houses on a street. The houses all belong to the same class, but within that class they have unique features. One house's garden faces South and gets more run. Another might have been painted an unusual colour by a previous owner. They are all houses on the same street, but their unique characteristics differentiate them, indeed making some more valuable than others.

ERC-721: The NFT Token Standard

ERC-721 is the token standard for creating non-fungible tokens on the Ethereum blockchain. The terms NFT and ERC-721 are often used interchangeably within the Ethereum community. Let's examine ERC-721 in relation to its most common usage, the Profile Picture (PFP) project, but keep in the back of our minds that it is just one of many potential use cases. The 10,000 PFP concept originates with the Cryptopunks collection (launched June 2017). Cryptopunks was created by Matt Hall and John Watkinson under the company name Larva Labs. The punks are simple 24 × 24 pixel images that were procedurally generated using an automated script. Note that this step does not require the Ethereum blockchain but might use a Python script to produce the actual images. The logic of the Cryptopunks script was designed to combine various traits – mohawks, eye patches, red hair, etc. – into a simple pixelated image of a face with punky features. Importantly, the script also established how common some traits are and how rare others are. For example, there are only 9 punks in the alien style, making them exceptionally rare. Cryptopunks precede the ERC-721 standard, but it is their popularity that really made clear the need for a general standard. The alternative would be custom smart contracts and token types for each project and this would make interoperability with marketplaces, for instance, a little clunky. By January 2018, a set of Ethereum enthusiasts – William Entriken, Dieter Shirley, Jacob Evans and Nastassia Sachs – published their standard for non-fungible tokens, ERC-721.[1]

ERC-721 PFP smart contracts are designed with the following goals in mind:

a The launch parameters, including the date of the mint and the initial cost of the NFTs.
b Information about the project, such as the project's name, the scarcity of the items or the location of images and metadata.
c Functions people can call.
d The post-launch mapping of which EOA user account currently owns which NFT.

To achieve all this, an ERC-721 smart contract is a collection of functions. Functions are pieces of code in a smart contract that perform a certain task. The functions can be called by EOAs that want to interact with the smart contract. For example, when the project launches you can call the function *name* and it will return a stored piece of text (a *string*) with the name Bored Ape Yacht Club. Or you might call the function *totalSupply* and it will return a number telling you how many Bored Apes exist (as an unsigned integer, *unit256*). However, in these cases, we're really just pulling information from the smart contract account on Ethereum. The more impactful functions are those that cause a state transition or change in the state of the Ethereum world computer. For example, when BAYC launched, an EOA could create a transaction called the *mintApe* function in the BAYC smart contract. This transaction required the EOA to send 0.08 ETH to mint a Bored Ape. If my transactions are legitimate, the NFT was transferred to my EOA wallet software. I am now the proud owner of a Bored Ape NFT! Once minted the NFT is under control of the EOA. The EOA can transfer the token to other people or list it for sale on a marketplace. When the initial mint is over, most NFT smart contracts are indexing current NFT ownership or granting permission for marketplaces to list NFTs for sale on behalf of the EOA.

The Properties of an NFT

The question you might be asking is what *precisely* is an NFT? If we examine an ERC-721 smart contract we'll see a list of functions users can call. Within the functions, we can see some terms indicating important properties of an NFT.

TokenId: A *TokenId* is a number identifying an NFT.

TokenURI: A *TokenURI* is a link pointing to the location of the metadata and image associated with a TokenId. URI stands for Uniform Resource Identifier. It's similar to the idea of a URL link.

The metadata: The actual metadata (e.g. traits) including the image that the TokenURI points to. The metadata is usually stored off-chain. The most popular storage choices are the Peer-to-Peer (P2P) InterPlanetary File System (IPFS) storage protocol or the storage-customised blockchain known as Arweave. But don't be surprised to find a link to Amazon Web Services (AWS).

An NFT is a combination of all three properties. It is the unique reference number (TokenId), the link to the metadata stored on-chain (TokenURI) and finally the actual metadata, usually stored off-chain: *TokenId* + *TokenURI* + *metadata* = NFT.

In some cases, but not all, this data gets hashed into what is called the *provenance record*. The *provenance record* is a hash constructed from the collective hashes of the individual NFTs in a project. This is useful because if the project owners decide to meddle with the metadata then the provenance hash will change.

Let's illustrate all this with an example. By far the most popular use of the ERC-721 token standard for NFTs is the 10,000 PFP collection. The PFP model was popularised in the mainstream imagination by the Bored Ape Yacht Club (BAYC) collection (launched in April 2021). BAYC was created by Greg Solano (Gargamel) and Wylie Aronow (Gordon Goner) under the company name Yuga Labs.[2] Similar to Cryptopunks, each Bored Ape was procedurally generated but is based on original artwork. Like Cryptopunks, the idea is that the Bored Apes have unique traits, with some relatively common and others quite rare. The smart contract follows the broad ERC-721 template, with some modifications. Each Bored Ape has a TokenID and a TokenURI with a pointer to the metadata stored on IPFS, where the image is stored. The provenance record is a long table of each individual NFT's important information: sequence placement, TokenID, TokenURI and IPFS link. The contract contains all the core information you need: project name, ticker, how many Bored Apes there are, etc. For the sale, the contract set a 0.08 ETH mint price and randomised what Bored Apes mint and when.[3] In total, 30 Bored Apes were set aside for the creators. Once the sale ended and all the Bored Apes were sold, the BAYC smart contract tracks the transfer of Bored Apes between EOA user accounts and grants permissions for listings. The BAYC smart contract stipulates a 2.5% royalty fee on any future sales of Bored Apes on marketplaces, creating a revenue stream for Yuga Labs.

The Commercial and Legal Side of NFTs

NFT marketplaces bring together NFT collections and collectors who wish to trade with each other. An EOA user account that connects to an NFT marketplace will be able to list their NFTs for sale or search for new ones to purchase. The marketplace will pull collection information from the NFT project's smart contract account on Ethereum and display it in a user-friendly format, including pulling the metadata from the TokenURI, such as the image. The most popular NFT marketplace for many years was Opensea, but its market share has been challenged increasingly over the years by upstart challengers such as Blur and X2Y2. Marketplaces charge sellers a fee for sales, e.g. Opensea has a 2.5% fee on sales. Here it is important to stress again we are discussing the broadest model of NFT creation and sales. Fee structures vary from market to market, including whether creator royalties are paid or not.

The legal status of NFTs remains an open discussion. The most common issues that arise are around Intellectual Property (IP). IP has a number of dimensions and we expect to see many interesting NFT court cases in the coming years. The first dimension to be aware of is copyright. Copyright emerges around something that is original, creative and involves human authorship. For example, BAYC is an original concept, it is creative, and human effort lies behind the base artwork, the generative script and the smart contract creation. Interestingly, copyright is not the same as copyright registration. Copyright is established automatically when a novel and creative project is launched. Copyright registration is a US-specific process that does help to enforce copyright in the US, but lacking it does not mean a project does not have copyright in general. BAYC does not have copyright registration, but is understood to have copyright over the BAYC Intellectual Property (IP). BAYC grants Bored Ape owners commercial rights to use the NFT. Bored Ape holders can make t-shirts or open a bar with their Bored Ape as part of the theme (and both of these have happened). If you intend to become a serious NFT collector then it is important to understand what rights buying the NFT might confer. Some are quite rigid, some are quite open.

Notes

1 The creation of ERC-721 is partly tied up with the creation of the CryptoKitties NFT collection (launched in December 2017).
2 Note here that Cryptopunks (Larva Labs) and BAYC (Yuga Labs) are both collections made by traditional companies. In fact, Yuga Labs acquired the IP for Cryptopunks from Larva Labs in 2022. Thus while there are many individual or organic community NFT projects there are a lot of just traditional company-type models.
3 At least in theory. It didn't actually do this in the end! But that was the intent.

8 Ethereum Layer 2 and the Roadmap

Over its history, Ethereum researchers have proposed different solutions to scaling (e.g. state channels, plasma channels), but have converged on rollups as the broad solution. There are two main types of rollup: optimistic and zero-knowledge. Both broadly follow the logic of separating execution into Layer 2s, but then settling the results on Ethereum Layer 1. Until quite recently, rollups were seen as a future solution, but a number of them have already launched and many others are close to launch. Many users, including myself, spend much of their time on Layer 2s rather than Layer 1 and in the future this will likely be commonplace. Alongside the rollup-centric vision, we find the Ethereum Roadmap. The Roadmap outlines the long-term plans of Ethereum developers and researchers. It is not a static roadmap, but more a semi-formal open-ended set of targets that are likely to evolve over time. However, the hope is that at some stage, when the major goals are completed, Ethereum will enter its "endgame," where the protocol ossifies and is eclipsed as an infrastructure behind the many innovative dApps built upon it. In this chapter, I presume strong familiarity with everything we have discussed so far, since these topics are all highly advanced and cannot be approached without foundational knowledge of Ethereum.

The Scalability Trilemma

Ethereum's creator, Vitalik Buterin, introduced the Scalability Trilemma to capture how blockchains struggle to achieve three desirable properties of a blockchain: scalability, decentralisation and security. The trilemma relates to how a blockchain can usually combine two of the properties well, but usually at the expense of the third.

Scalability: how many transactions per second (tps) can be processed.
Decentralisation: how decentralised the blockchain is, measured in nodes.
Security: how resistant the blockchain is to attack.

DOI: 10.4324/9781003319603-8

Bitcoin and Ethereum are examples of blockchains with high degrees of decentralisation and security, but limited scalability. Both blockchains have thousands of full nodes and miners/validators, making them decentralised, and both have either large amounts of computational power (Bitcoin) or staked ETH (Ethereum) that secure them. However, for Ethereum, the sheer number of nodes and staked ETH means we can only realistically share a certain amount of transactions to be processed by full nodes and validators. Due to these constraints, Ethereum Layer 1 can process about 15 transactions per second. We could, in theory, sacrifice decentralisation and security by limiting consensus to a small number of centralised nodes. But, of course, that's not desirable to the Ethereum community. It is clear, then, that we must find a way to have scalability while keeping decentralisation and security. In the very long term, and it really depends on whether it's required, Ethereum might implement sharding, where Ethereum Layer 1 is broken into shards that validators will work on in parallel. In the immediate term, the rollup-centric Layer 2 vision has become the vision.

Rollups

Ethereum Mainnet is known as Layer 1. It is the main Ethereum blockchain we have come to know and love. Rollups are known as Layer 2s. They separate execution to a Layer 2, but settle on Layer 1. The Layer 2 processes transactions in its own EVM and stores a rollup world state. At intervals, the transactions on the Layer 2 are bundled into a single transaction and sent to Layer 1 for settlement. In this manner, Layer 2s are said to "inherit" the security of Ethereum because ultimately that is where Layer 2 transactions are settled. Rollups alleviate the pressure on Layer 1 by creating an alternative venue for transactions. Due to the highly efficient use of gas by Layer 2 rollups, gas fees for the end user are quite small relative to Layer 1.

Optimistic Rollups

Optimistic rollups are composed of a smart contract on Ethereum Layer 1 and a rollup on Layer 2. The Layer 1 smart contract facilitates the communication between layers. Typically, a user will deposit assets into the rollup's Layer 1 smart contract and then the assets are bridged over to the Layer 2 rollup. In turn, a user can also exit the rollup by bridging back to Layer 1. Once bridged over, transactions on the optimistic rollup are sent to a sequencer. Sequencers are rollup entities that process incoming transactions. Transactions are bundled into a block, but in a highly optimised form. The sequencer submits the block to Layer 1 as Call Data. Remember, Call Data is the Input Data field in a transaction.

By placing all transactions together into the Call Data, many rollup transactions can be treated as one Layer 1 transaction. The transaction submitted to Layer 1 also includes the old State Root and the newly proposed State Root caused by the transactions. The reason we call them optimistic rollups is because the new State Root is presumed to be honest and to only contain legitimate transactions. However, once sent to Layer 1 there is a challenge period. If there is a discrepancy between the Layer 1 and Layer 2 State Roots, the challenged transaction is re-executed. The most popular Layer 2 optimistic rollups are Arbitrum, Optimism, Base and Linea.

Zero-Knowledge Rollups

Zero-knowledge (ZK) rollups follow the same broad model found in optimistic rollups, but with an important tweak. There is a smart contract on Layer 1 and the ability to bridge over to the Layer 2 zero-knowledge rollup. Once there, a user submits transactions to a sequencer, who bundles many transactions into a single transaction to be posted to Layer 1 as Call Data. However, rather than a challenge period, ZK rollups include a validity proof. Validity proofs are cryptographic assurances that the state transition processed by the rollup is legitimate. Validity proofs can be verified immediately, rather than requiring a challenge period. The most popular Layer 2 zero-knowledge rollups are zkSync and Starknet.

The Ethereum Roadmap

The Ethereum Roadmap is a semi-formal set of objectives that Ethereum developers and researchers are working toward.[1] It reflects the major goals the researcher and development community believe will solve any outstanding problems in the Ethereum protocol. It acts like a checklist of desirable solutions to be formalised into EIPs and then included in future upgrades. There is no clear-cut answer to how long the Roadmap will take to complete, but we are talking in the region of 5–10 years. At some stage, it is hoped the protocol will ossify into a generally accepted state where no major changes are needed, but this depends, of course, on no unforeseen issues emerging. The nature of book publishing means some of these will likely already be part of the Ethereum protocol when you are reading this.

The Roadmap has six areas to tackle. These are The Merge (consensus mechanism), The Surge (Scaling), The Scourge (centralisation risks), The Verge (block verification), The Purge (cleaning up the protocol) and The Splurge (everything else). I've picked some highlights that are expected in the near-term future, but people with a strong interest in Ethereum's future should check out the full roadmap. Since research into most of these topics is at an early stage, I can only really describe their intent, rather than how they will be implemented. Remember, these are just some near-term highlights and each area has much wider ambitions long term.

Single Leader Selection/Single Slot Finality (The Merge)

Currently, block proposers are known in advance. There is limited public information about full nodes, but IP addresses can be exposed. An adversary might use this information to engage in malicious behaviour, such as a Denial of Service (DoS) attack that disrupts the block proposer during their slot. *Secret leader selection* is a research aim where only block proposers know they have been selected for a slot. Another proposed improvement to consensus is *Single Slot Finality*, which will allow blocks to be finalised immediately.

Proto-danksharding (EIP 4844) (The Surge)

Proto-danksharding (EIP 4844) will replace the current method of rollups posting transaction information as Call Data. When rollups send the Call Data to Layer 1, it needs to be processed and added to the blockchain, where it is stored permanently. However, rollups only need transaction data temporarily, during the time period when they can be challenged. Proto-danksharding introduces a new way to store rollup data, called blobs, that will be stored only for as long as required (likely 1–3 months) and then discarded.

Proposer-Builder Separation (PBS) (The Scourge)

Proposer-Builder Separation (PBS) formalises the distinct roles of proposer and builder. PBS has always been intended to become enshrined as part of the Ethereum protocol, but it took a back seat to the transition from mining to staking, The Merge. Into this gap, MEV-Boost emerged as a solution that enabled block builders to build execution blocks that then get passed on to relays, who in turn aggregate them and allow block proposers to choose the most profitable. Once PBS is added, proposers will no longer optionally build blocks themselves, but only block builders will. In effect, PBS legitimates the role of the block builder into the Ethereum protocol, rather than the quasi-official situation they exist in now.

Account Abstraction (The Splurge)

Externally-Owned Accounts (EOA) are a little clunky in design. They more or less just allow users to create transactions and call functions from contract accounts. *Account abstraction* will either enable EOAs to be managed by smart contracts or enable smart contracts to create transactions, like an EOA does now. This should allow for major improvements in the user experience, such as social recovery of private keys, batched transactions, security rules, etc. Overall, account abstraction should bring the user account experience more in line with what everyday users expect when they hear the words "user account."

Conclusion

I leave you, dear reader, I hope, with more knowledge than you came in with. There are no doubt many areas you feel you know only obliquely and that is normal enough with Ethereum. Many people in Ethereum speak of the experience of a rabbit hole. Every time you think you've found the end there's another twist and turn. Ever more to learn. At first, this feels daunting, like you can't possibly master it all. What this means, in practice, is that you pick and choose the part of the rabbit hole you enjoy and specialise in it. The trick is to realise that the deepness of the rabbit hole is not a formidable opponent, but an opportunity. Everywhere in Ethereum, there is a place where you can make a contribution. Everywhere there is a place where you can be among the first explorers of the frontier. To those pondering what to do next, I suggest contributing to the ethereum.org website. It's an open-source volunteer community where the content is produced by, well, anyone. No coding is required, just the ability to learn about and then communicate Ethereum concepts. And always remember, to paraphrase Jameson Lopp about Bitcoin, "nobody understands Ethereum and that's OK!"

Note

1 The Roadmap as posted by Vitalik Buterin on Twitter: https://twitter.com/VitalikButerin/status/1588669782471368704/photo/1

Appendix
Introduction to Bitcoin

Bitcoin is a decentralised money system. You can imagine Bitcoin as a shared digital ledger tracking a currency, bitcoins. What makes Bitcoin unique is how no single entity controls the ledger. Instead, the ledger is maintained in an open, collaborative manner. Bitcoin uses blockchain technology to achieve this goal. A blockchain is a secure digital record-keeping system that enables decentralised coordination among users. Bitcoin has three core components – network, identity and consensus – that combine to secure its blockchain. This introduction to Bitcoin is highly truncated and written in the context of an introductory book on Ethereum. The topics here, and the many omitted, deserve their own chapters and I recommend that Bitcoin enthusiasts consult the many specialist books written on Bitcoin.

Bitcoin Network

Bitcoin is, at heart, an open-source volunteer project. The Bitcoin open-source community orbits around a software client called Bitcoin Core that expresses the Bitcoin protocol or ruleset. When a user runs the Bitcoin Core software, they connect to other users running the same software, forming a network. Since this network is composed of connected peers – users running the client software – it is called a Peer-to-Peer (P2P) network. What is unusual in this scenario is that there is no central point in the network, no central peer. In the Bitcoin network, everyone is following the same protocol about a currency. The primary unit of this currency is 1 bitcoin (BTC), which can be subdivided into 100,000,000 Satoshis (or sats). A sat is 0.00000001 bitcoin. Bitcoin users running the full software, including hosting copies of the complete digital ledger, are known as full nodes. Not all Bitcoin users are full nodes. In fact, most are not. Many use Simplified Payment Verification (SPV) wallets. SPV wallets rely on full nodes for the latest state of the Bitcoin network and come in many forms: lightweight Desktop wallets, browser extensions, websites, mobile wallets, hardware wallets etc. Many users, unfortunately, don't even use their own software but instead keep their bitcoins on centralised exchanges. Since the Bitcoin network is distributed across thousands of full nodes, it is exceptionally difficult to shut down the network. An adversary would need to locate each full node instance and shut them down, an unrealistic scenario.

Bitcoin Identity

Public Key Cryptography is used to establish pseudonymous identities in Bitcoin. When you download Bitcoin software, a key pair identity is created for you. This key pair includes a private key and a public key. These keys are cryptographically related. The private key, which should never be revealed to anyone, is what establishes ownership of bitcoins. It is an imperfect analogy, but a private key is *like* (but not the same as) the password to your online accounts, except losing your private key is the same as losing access to your bitcoins. There's no password reset button or company to complain to. The associated public key can be shared with anyone and will be used to verify transactions you send.

A private key is a number between 1 and 2^{256} (a 256-bit number). This is an astronomical range and no two people are likely to arrive at the same one. Since your private key is a number, it can be represented in many different ways. For example, here is a representation of a private key produced by the Bitcoin Core software:

L34ENboLf2h2uNkpNW8pMcJ2cFixRmsUDiHW2m8pucfa1p4z
YmGd

The format and how your private keys will be stored will depend on your software. A popular variation, albeit one absent in Bitcoin Core, is to derive a set of private keys from a seed phrase or mnemonic. Your identity is not tied to any specific wallet. You can import your private key to any Bitcoin wallet software.

Your public key is derived from the private key. A public key is a set of coordinates cryptographically related to the private key. The public key of the private key above is:

0325CCF70B20522B0E68A3FB31B94986364267B9D217638I5DBB
89F32C9AE8DCC3

To receive bitcoins, we generate Bitcoin addresses. Bitcoin addresses are derived from public keys and are used to receive bitcoins. A public address looks as follows:

1PHeNJGuYyY5R9JEEDUef78RzJXpLWxS1W

Public key cryptography enables a digital signature scheme in Bitcoin. The logic is as follows:

a Generate a private key.
b Generate the associated public key.
c Generate address from public key.
d Sign transactions with a digital signature using private key.
e Verify digital signatures using public key.

Bitcoin Transactions

Let's imagine a Bitcoin transaction in practice. We can envisage a user called Alice (sender) and another called Bob (recipient). Alice's wallet software tracks all the bitcoins she has received in the past, that she controls with private keys. In Bitcoin, a user's balance is all the unspent bitcoins they have previously received. In technical terms, all the bitcoins you receive are called Unspent Transaction Outputs (UTXOs). A UTXO is just a denomination of bitcoin (say 0.1 or 5.2) and an owner. The Bitcoin network is, at any one time, a snapshot of all these Unpent Transaction Outputs (the UTXO set) and who can currently spend them. I'll speak plainly of sending and receiving bitcoins.

Bitcoin transactions transfer bitcoins from one owner to another. In our example, Alice wants to send Bob 100 bitcoin and she has in the past received this amount. When Alice starts a transaction, her software will find bitcoins she can spend. Alice's unspent bitcoins are the inputs for the transaction. If she can't find the exact amount received, the wallet software will aggregate from smaller amounts or else overpay and receive a change (to a change address). Alice will also attach a transaction fee to pay the users who maintain the Bitcoin blockchain. Once the transaction is complete, the 100 bitcoins are unspent bitcoins for Bob. Bob can now use these in future transactions.

To validate Alice's transaction, Bitcoin uses a simple programming language for the unlocking and locking of unspent bitcoins called Script (created by Nakamoto). I'll use the most common example. scriptPubKey is a locking script placed on sent bitcoins determining the conditions they can be spent under. When Alice sends Bob bitcoins she is really telling the network, by way of scriptPubKey, how these bitcoins can be spent in the future. In this case, the locking script stipulates: to spend these bitcoins, the recipient must provide a digital signature from the private key associated with the public key the bitcoins were locked to. Bob in the future can then unlock these received bitcoins using the corresponding scriptSig unlocking script. And likely Bob will then be locking those bitcoins to someone else's public key, for them to unlock later.

Bitcoin Consensus

Transactions in the Bitcoin network are recorded on the Bitcoin blockchain. The blockchain is Bitcoin's ledger tracking the balances of all users. Remember, in Bitcoin, there is no central authority responsible for the upkeep of this ledger. Instead, there is a subset of the Bitcoin community known as miners who undertake this role. Originally almost all Bitcoin users were miners, but today it is a specialist role. Miners are tasked with bundling transactions together into blocks, like a page in a ledger. Every ten minutes, one miner among many will be selected to append the next block to the blockchain ledger. A block is a data structure containing all the important information the Bitcoin network keeps track of.

The body of the block is a list of the transactions. Blocks have an approximately 4MB limit. Block construction uses cryptographic hashing extensively. Hash functions are algorithms that take input data of arbitrary size and output fixed-length hashes. Below I have taken the word Bitcoin as input and put it through a hash function to generate a hash:

b4056df6691f8dc72e56302ddad345d65fead3ead9299609a826e2344eb 63aa4

If I alter any data the hash changes. Here is bitcoin in lower case:

6b88c087247aa2f07ee1c5956b8e1a9f4c7f892a70e324f1bb3d161e05ca 107b

Bitcoin uses the SHA-256 hash function to produce short digests of data with this method and puts it to work in structuring blocks. Blocks have a block header containing contextual information about the blockchain and then a block body that contains the transactions list. The block header is quite important in Bitcoin. It looks as follows:

Version:	Software/protocol version.
Prev Hash:	Hash of the previous block.
Merkle Root:	Hash summary of transactions.
Timestamp:	Block time.
Difficulty:	Proof of Work difficulty.
Nonce:	A number used in the Proof of Work solution.

Prev Hash is a hash of the previous block added to the canonical blockchain. We can also see a Merkle Root. The Merkle Root is a hash summary of the transaction list. Each new block will embed Prev Hash (which includes the last block's Merkle Root) into its block header and thereby create a cryptographic link with the last, which in turn links to the one before it and all the way back to the first block, known as the Genesis block. If anyone tries to re-create a past block with new data, such as transaction data, the block's hash would change and be easily recognisable to the Bitcoin network as malicious behaviour.

We need to understand Bitcoin's mechanism for reaching consensus to understand the final field in the block header, the Nonce. Bitcoin's consensus mechanism is known as Proof of Work (PoW) or mining. I'll refer to Bitcoin mining. Let's look at a transaction as it makes its way to the miners. When transactions are sent in the Bitcoin network, full nodes verify whether the bitcoins are not already spent and the unlocking script conditions are satisfied (the correct digital signature appears with it). Once verified, these become unconfirmed transactions in the mempool, the "waiting room." Users running mining node software build their blocks from transactions in the mempool. We'll need a mechanism to select one miner to add their block to the blockchain because a ledger must be a single ledger or it makes no sense. But how do we reach consensus about a ledger in the absence of a central authority?

Let's imagine the last block has just been added to the blockchain. Miners will typically have a candidate block ready, containing verified transactions from the mempool. They cannot, however, append their block right away. They are in competition with every other miner to append the next block and the competition will last approximately ten minutes. In order to be selected as the next block, miners must now provide a proof response to a challenge. The challenge is to produce a hash output that meets and satisfies certain conditions, known as the Difficulty. The Difficulty measures how difficult it is for miners to currently produce an acceptable hash output below a certain threshold or target. The challenge relies on another important quality of cryptographic hash functions. Hash functions are one-way or irreversible. Imagine, for example, I showed you the following hash with no context:

6d7b3f8ad28b16aa0f5a3128465be936c32a94f2ba8163dedc148654fa9e78a8

There is nothing in this hash output that allows you to work back logically to the input, which is the name Hal Finney, the first person to receive a Bitcoin transaction. Using this logic of unpredictability, the PoW mechanism challenges miners to find a hash that leads with a certain number of leading zeroes. The core of this challenge is that the hash output is in hexadecimal Base16 form (0–9, A–F). Asking a miner to hash an output with a single leading zero is therefore not too difficult and will require about 16 hashes. But asking them to produce a hash with 2 leading zeroes means it will require 16^2 hashes (about 256 hashes) and adding 3 leading zeroes will require 16^3 (about 4096 hashes) and so forth. It is therefore extremely difficult to find hashes with, for example, 20 leading zeroes. Miners cannot pre-hash their block. Miners need to integrate the latest Prev Hash of the latest block into their own block header. This Prev Hash is announced to everyone at roughly the same time when the last miner successfully finds it.

To produce an acceptable hash, miners take their block header and concatenate it with a Nonce (or number once). This combination is run through the SHA-256 hash function twice to produce potentially successful hashes. Since finding an acceptable hash is exceptionally difficult, the first hash will likely fail. The miner then increments the Nonce and tries a new block header and Nonce combination. When this fails they increment again. Miners will keep iterating until one miner is successful. At this point, the successful miner will present the block header and Nonce combination hash to the rest of the Bitcoin network. The nodes will verify that the combination does indeed produce an acceptable hash and the successful miner's block is added next to the blockchain. The miners all immediately move on to constructing a new candidate block and the mining process starts all over again.

The Difficulty is adjusted algorithmically every two weeks in response to how quickly miners are adding blocks. The network aims to produce blocks approximately every ten minutes, but it may deviate. This is because the hash rate, the cumulative amount of computational power mining at any one time, can fluctuate. Because more computational power means more hashes, the proof response will be found quicker, bringing down the block time. Conversely, when the hash rate decreases, the proof response may take longer, increasing the block time. Therefore the difficulty adjustment will reset the difficulty in response to the hash rate to ensure that a hash is found approximately every ten minutes. This is possible because while we cannot know what block header and combination in the input will succeed, we do know probabilistically how many hashes are needed to find a result. Demanding more zeros increases the difficulty, and demanding fewer decreases it.

When a miner finds an acceptable hash output and their block is appended to the blockchain, it increases the total amount of effort (Proof of Work hashing) that has gone into the blockchain. If two blocks are successfully proposed at once, uncommon but possible, then miners will keep both chains, but immediately select whatever one adds another block, because now this blockchain has the most cumulative Proof of Work.

Why do miners participate in this process? There is a special transaction at the top of the transaction list called the coinbase. The coinbase transaction sends the block reward to an address controlled by the successful mining node. The block reward is an amount of bitcoins rewarded to the successful mining node for adding a block to the blockchain. The original block reward was 50 bitcoins, but it halves every four years (25, 12.5 ...). It is currently 6.25 bitcoins per block. Miners also receive the transaction fees. The block reward is not just how miners are incentivised, but also how new bitcoins are generated or issued. Since the block reward halves every four years, there is a point in 2140 where no new bitcoins will be issued to miners. Instead, they will have to subsidise themselves on transaction fees. The diminishing reward schedule means there will only ever be 21 million bitcoins generated. Nakamoto hoped to mimic in digital form the properties of gold, which is a scarce resource that people expend effort to find, hence the term mining.

Originally, miners could use the Central Processing Unit (CPU) on their home computers and laptops. However, miners quickly realised they could use their Graphics Processing Units (GPUs) to produce faster hashes. This eventually led to the creation of specialist hardware known as Application Specific Integrated Circuits (ASICs). To compete today, a small miner will typically combine their hash rate with others in a mining pool and share the rewards. The huge amount of computational power pointed at the Bitcoin mining consensus mechanism means Bitcoin is very difficult to attack. An adversary would need to accumulate enough hash rate to overpower all the other miners, a 51% attack. This would be extremely expensive and economically irrational since a miner with such a large amount of hash rate would be better off acting honestly and winning the block reward and fees.

There is, naturally, much more to Bitcoin than covered here, including important historical moments such as the Bitcoin Civil War (2015–2017) and technical improvements, such as Lightning Network, but this should prove enough foundation to tackle those more complicated topics in the many books published on Bitcoin.

Glossary

Arbitrageurs   traders who take advantage of price discrepancies across exchanges, whether centralised or decentralised.

Architectural decentralisation   blockchains are distributed among all full node participants, rather than located in a single place.

Archival node   a full node that includes the complete history of the blockchain and does not prune.

Attestation   a vote in the staking consensus mechanism. Validators attest to the head of the blockchain, to the target checkpoint and to the source checkpoint.

Automated Market Makers (AMMs)   smart contract protocols for swapping ERC-20 assets.

Base fee   refers to the algorithmically dynamic cost of gwei in the Ethereum network.

Beacon block   contains contextual information about the consensus mechanism, such as proposer, validators, attestations, deposits, etc. Built by the block proposer in a slot.

Beacon Chain   Ethereum's consensus blockchain containing the history of Ethereum and extended block by block to reflect new activity.

Beacon Root   hash of the Beacon state.

Beacon state   the state of the Beacon Chain.

Block   data structures containing contextual information about a blockchain. The block headers contain high-level information and the block body usually contains more complete information.

Block builders   construct and format blocks that include optimised MEV transactions.

Blockchain   a secure digital record-keeping system that enables decentralised coordination among users.

Blockchain culture   the social, cultural or political values shared by a blockchain community.

Blockchain economies   the economic and financial activity associated with a blockchain implementation.

Blockchain governance the coordination mechanisms that allow blockchain stakeholders to make legitimate decisions about the protocol.

Blockchain oracles third-party or middleware services that provide external or off-chain data to the blockchain.

Blockchain stakeholders are groups with a stake or interest, whether financial or cultural, in a blockchain implementation.

Block proposer the specific validator who has been chosen during a slot to build a block.

BLS signatures the digital signature scheme used by validators. Has the specific quality of fast verification when aggregated.

Borrowing/lending platforms smart contract protocols that enable users to borrow and lend Crypto assets.

Bridges enable cross-chain transfers between blockchains.

Call Data the content of the Input Data field in a transaction.

Casper the Friendly Finality Gadget (Casper-FFG) the attestation to two checkpoints that results in the justification and then finalisation of a point on the blockchain.

Centralisation the concentration of decision-making in an organisation or industry to a single authority or a small set of authorities.

Centralised exchange trading platforms for Crypto assets run by companies.

Checkpoint refers to two blocks attested to at the start of epochs. The more immediate is called the target and the one prior is called the source. There also exists weak subjectivity checkpoints that mark points in the blockchain that are generally agreed upon as incontrovertible.

Client diversity designed to ensure that any issues found in one client don't impact the entire network.

Committees groups of attesting validators assigned to validate a slot.

Consensus mechanism an incentivised protocol a blockchain uses to reach agreement on a state of affairs.

Contract accounts smart contracts that have been deployed on Ethereum and are controlled by their own internal code.

Contract Creation a transaction that requests a new contract account to be added to the Ethereum world state.

Contributors highly engaged members that belong to one or more workstreams in a DAO.

Decentralised Exchange (DEX) an umbrella term for DeFi smart contract protocols that allow users to swap Crypto assets.

Decentralised Application (dApp) a smart contract plus the non-blockchain technologies it combines with to aid the user experience.

Decentralised Autonomous Organisations (DAOs) communities that self-organise using blockchain technology. In practice, commonly operated in conjunction or relation with a company, often one that progressively decentralised into a DAO-company hybrid structure.

Decentralised Finance (DeFi) an ecosystem of protocols that enable permissionless and transparent finance.

Delegates DAO members who vote on behalf of DAO token holders.

Deposit contract a list of participating validators.

Derivatives Exchanges smart contract protocols allowing users to trade complex financial instruments like perpetual futures, options, etc.

Digital signature cryptographic signature appended to transactions using private keys.

Eek 2048 epochs or approximately 9.1 days.

Epoch a measurement of time on the Beacon chain. 32 slots long or approximately 6.4 minutes.

ERC-20 the token standard for creating currencies or tokens on the Ethereum blockchain.

ERC-721 the token standard for creating non-fungible tokens on the Ethereum blockchain.

Ether (ETH) Ethereum's native asset.

Ethereum addresses 42-character hexadecimal identifiers derived from the last 20 bytes of the public key using cryptographic hash functions, with a short 0x prefix added.

Ethereum network made up of full nodes that together form a Peer-to-Peer (P2P) network.

Ethereum protocol an overarching name for the various technical specifications found in Ethereum, such as the white paper, yellow paper and the Execution and Consensus Layer specs.

Ethereum wallet software allowing Ethereum users to manage an account or wallet. Distinct from a full node.

Ethereum Virtual Machine (EVM) the Central Processing Unit (CPU) that coordinates the transition of the Ethereum world state.

EVM bytecode the low-level programming language the EVM can read and execute.

EVM Memory temporary memory used during the State Transition Function (or machine state) to track changes.

Execution block contains the execution payload in a block data structure. The execution block is nested within the Beacon block.

Execution Layer (EL) names the part of the Ethereum protocol concerned with executing transactions.

Execution payload an output summary of the EVM's state transition function.

Externally Owned Account (EOA) user accounts that can create transactions and are controlled by private keys.

Finality once a source checkpoint is finalised, the preceding blocks are considered permanent and cannot be reverted, achieving finality.

Flash loan   an uncollateralised loan that takes place within a single block, usually knitting together a series of complex smart contract interactions that take advantage of an arbitrage opportunity.

Forks   chain splits that can be unintentional or malicious or else intentionally used to upgrade the protocol.

Frontrunning   when a searcher identifies a profitable trade from another user and then displaces it with their own, paying a higher gas fee.

Full node   a user with a complete copy (albeit pruned) of the blockchain and capable of verifying transactions, the world state and the blockchain record. Requires an execution and consensus client. The backbone of the Ethereum network.

Gas cost   every Opcode a transaction requires has an associated gas cost.

Gas counter   tracks the gas used during the EVM's state transition. Reverts if no more gas is available and undoes the proposed state changes.

Gas fees   a small denomination of ETH called gwei (one billion wei or 0.0000000001 ETH) used to pay for the gas costs of a transaction.

Gas Limit (transaction)   the maximum amount of gas, that is units of computation, a user is willing to pay for.

Gas Limit (block)   caps the overall amount of gas used in a block.

Gasper   the name used when referring to LMD-GHOST and Casper-FFG together.

Governance tokens   confer membership and voting rights to DAO participants.

Hash functions   algorithms that take input data of arbitrary size and output fixed-length hashes.

Impermanent loss   when a liquidity provider would have been better off holding an asset than supplying it to a pool.

Inactivity leak penalty   a contingency mechanism that kicks in when a large percentage of validators are failing to perform their duties.

Initial Coin Offering (ICO)   a fundraising mechanism where users send ETH to a contract in exchange for a project's newly created token.

Liquidity mining   the act of providing assets to liquidity pools in exchange for transaction fees.

Liquidity Pools (LPs)   smart contracts holding Crypto assets for use in Decentralised Exchanges (DEXs).

Liveness   the desired property of adding blocks quickly to slots to keep the blockchain moving along or "live."

LMD GHOST   Latest Message Driven (LMD) Greedy Heaviest-Observed Sub-Tree (GHOST) attestation to the latest block at the head of the blockchain.

Maximum Extractable Value (MEV)   refers to the extracting of value by manipulating how transactions are ordered within a block.

Mempool the waiting room of transactions waiting to be processed prior to inclusion in a block. The mempool is not a single place, but rather each full node has a mempool that they can build upon, if acting as a block proposer (or block builder).

Merkle Patricia Trie a data structure that allows important information to be accessed securely and efficiently.

Message Calls transactions from EOAs communicating a desired change in the Ethereum world state.

NFT marketplaces bring together NFT collections and collectors who wish to trade with each other.

Non-Fungible Tokens (NFTs) digital tokens that represent unique assets on a blockchain.

Opcode an instruction or command to be processed by the EVM.

Open source a development process where volunteers work collaboratively to make non-proprietary software.

Oracle problem the problem of communicating information between the blockchain and the external world.

Peer-to-Peer (P2P) networking a technique where individual computers, known as nodes, connect with other computers and contribute toward some shared goal. Each node is equal to one another. There is no central point in the network.

Political decentralisation authority is spread among all participating members, rather than concentrated.

Price impact the differences in prices that come from swaps, especially large ones that tilt the ratio in an AMM.

Price slippage the difference between expected price and actual price when using an AMM.

Priority fee an additional amount of gwei a user can pay above the base fee to hopefully get processed faster.

Program Counter tracks what instructions from the contract code that need to be processed next by the EVM.

Progressive decentralisation the model of transitioning from a company or corporate structure into a Decentralised Autonomous Organisation (DAO), whether in part or completely.

Provenance record a hash constructed from the collective hashes of the individual NFTs in a project.

Public Key Cryptography used to establish pseudonymous identities in a blockchain implementation.

Receipts Root a hash of the transaction receipts, the outcomes of processed transactions.

Relays passes builder blocks onto the block proposer.

Searchers users who watch the mempool for transactions that they can format into MEV opportunities, usually using automated bots to identify them.

Slashing   the penalty for a validator engaging in malicious behaviour.

Slot   a measurement of time on the Beacon chain. A slot is 12 seconds long.

Smart contract   a set of instructions called Opcodes written in EVM bytecode. The smart contract is then deployed as a contract account where it can be interacted with.

Stablecoin   a cryptocurrency or token that is pegged one-to-one with a fiat currency, such as the US dollar or Euro.

Stack   the EVM uses a stack-based model for executing code.

Staking pools   combine smaller amounts of ETH to create shared validators.

Slashing   the penalty for a validator engaging in malicious behaviour.

Slashing reward   a reward for reporting malicious behaviour.

State Root   a hash of the world state produced by hashing all the sub-items in the world state together: EOAs, contract accounts, contract account Storage.

State Transition Function   refers to the various operations that move Ethereum from state to state.

Storage (contract account)   maps the contents of the contract accounts.

Storage (EVM)   once transaction instructions are processed, they cause a change in the state of the contract account. These changes are recorded permanently to reflect the new world state that will emerge from the machine state.

Subnet   used to produce aggregate signatures for attestations.

Sync committee   validators assigned to provide block header information to light clients.

Tamper resistant   no single entity can unilaterally make changes to a blockchain's history.

TokenId   a number identifying an NFT in a smart contract.

Token holder   a DAO member who has the right to vote or participate in governance due to ownership of the DAO's governance

TokenURI   a pointer to the location of the metadata and image associated with a TokenId. URI stands for Uniform Resource Identifier. It's similar to the idea of a URL link.

Total Value Locked (TVL)   the total amount of value associated with a DeFi protocol.

Transactions Root   a hash of the transactions list.

Transparency   all activity that happens on a blockchain is completely public.

Trusted third party   an intermediary that users rely on to provide certain services.

Validator   an account with 32 ETH deposited to the deposit contract as collateral (the stake) in order to participate in consensus.

Validator set   the cumulative amount of validators currently involved in staking.

Virtual Read-Only Memory (ROM)   reads (but does not overwrite) the code of an involved contract account during the EVM's state transition.

Withdrawals Root   hash of the withdrawals list.

Workstream   a sub-unit within a DAO dedicated to a specific set of tasks, such as marketing, governance, community, etc.

World state   maps Ethereum addresses to EOAs or contract accounts.

Yield farming   when a user moves between different liquidity pools to chase the best yield.

Index

Note: Page numbers followed by "n" refer to notes.

Printed in the United States
by Baker & Taylor Publisher Services